General editor: Graham Hand

C000047035

Brodie's Notes on Barry I

Kes (a Kestrel for a Knave)

Graham Handley MA PhD
Formerly Principal Lecturer in English, College of All Saints, Tottenham

Pan Books London, Sydney and Auckland

Extracts from A Kestrel for a Knave
© Barry Hines 1968
Reproduced by permission of Michael Joseph Ltd
This revised edition published 1987 by Pan Books Ltd,
Cavaye Place, London SW10 9PG
9 8 7 6 5 4 3 2
© Graham Handley 1987
ISBN 0 330 50252 2
Photoset by Parker Typesetting Service, Leicester
Printed and bound in Great Britain by
Richard Clay Ltd, Bungay, Suffolk

Contents

Page references in these Notes are to the Penguin edition of *Kes* but as references are also given to particular sections, the Notes may be used with any edition of the book.

Preface

The intention throughout this study aid is to stimulate and guide, to encourage the reader's *involvement* in the text, to develop disciplined critical responses and a sure understanding of the main details.

Brodie's Notes provide a summary of the plot of the play or novel followed by act, scene or chapter summaries, each of which will have an accompanying critical commentary designed to emphasize the most important literary and factual details. Poems, stories or non-fiction texts will combine brief summary with critical commentary on either individual aspects or sequences of the genre being considered. Textual notes will be explanatory or critical (sometimes both), defining what is difficult or obscure on the one hand, or stressing points of character, style, plot or the technical aspects of poetry on the other. Revision questions will be set at appropriate points to test the student's careful application to the text of the prescribed book.

The second section of each of these study aids will consist of a critical examination of the author's art. This will cover such major elements as characterization, style, structure, setting, theme(s) for example in novels, plays or stories; in poetry it will deal with the types of poem, rhyme, rhythm, free verse for example, or in non-fiction with the main literary concerns of the work. The editor may choose to examine any aspect of the book being studied which he or she considers to be important. The paramount aim is to send the student back to the text. Each study aid will include a series of general questions which require detailed knowledge of the set book: the first of these questions will have notes by the editor of what *might* be included in a written answer. A short list of books considered useful as background reading for the student will be provided at the end.

The General Certificate of Secondary Education in Literature

These study aids are suitable for candidates taking the new GCSE examinations in English Literature since they provide detailed preparation for examinations in that subject as well as presenting critical ideas and commentary of major use to candidates preparing their coursework files. These aids provide a basic, individual and imaginative response to the appreciation of literature. They stimulate disciplined habits of reading, and they will assist the responsive student to analyse and to write about the texts with discrimination and insight.

Graham Handley

The author and his work

Barry Hines was born in a village near Barnsley in Yorkshire in 1939. He was educated at Ecclesfield Grammar School and had the distinction of playing for the England Grammar Schools Football team, later graduating, while doing various jobs, to the Barnsley 'A' team. Football has been and is one of the abiding loves of his life, and he still watches professional soccer regularly. He trained as a Physical Education teacher at Loughborough, taught for two years in London, and then returned to Yorkshire and settled down to teach there. He began to write, his first publication being *Billy's Last Stand* (1965), a play which has been produced on the radio, BBC television and on the stage. This was followed by *The Blinder* (1966), *A Kestrel for a Knave* (1968), *First Signs* (1972) and *The Gamekeeper* (1975). He also writes for television, and *Speech Day* (1973) made quite an impact as did *The Price of Coal* (1979). His most recent novel, *Looks and Smiles*, was filmed and won a prize at the Cannes Film Festival in 1981 and was televised in 1982. He held a fellowship at the University of Sheffield (1972–4) and later another creative arts post at Matlock College of Education. *A Kestrel for a Knave*, like Barry Hines's other work, speaks for itself, and this fine regional writer, who has returned to his roots, has given us a modern classic which I venture to say will not date with the passage of time.

Plot

The plot of *A Kestrel for a Knave* is succinct, straightforward, graphically immediate. A boy from a broken home, Billy Casper, living in somewhat deprived circumstances with a frequently drunken and aggressive brother and a free-living, irresponsible mother, seizes upon an individual outlet of compelling and unusual difference. The author uses a retrospective sequence to show us how Billy wandered beyond the confines of the estate to a nearby farm; there, despite an initial brush with the farmer, he discovers the nest of a kestrel, and later takes one of the young and rears it himself. He becomes, through sheer patience and fellow-feeling for the bird, an expert in his own small way, taking a loving pride in his achievement and in his relationship with the kestrel; these things are compensation for his abject homelife and the frustrations of school, where Billy is always in the wrong, the impoverished outsider in an unfriendly world.

But Billy goes too far in concern for his hawk. He provides beef for Kes which he has bought with his half-brother Jud's betting-money; some of that money goes on chips and scraps for himself, since he is so poorly fed at home that he is often reduced to reflex stealing. In school that afternoon Billy, looking out through the window, sees his brother appear, though he later manages to dodge him; when Billy returns home, he finds that Kes has gone. There follows an anguished and agonizing search, until the realization comes to Billy that his brother has killed the kestrel. Billy makes an impassioned and pathetic appeal to his mother to punish Jud for his terrible revenge, but his mother is, of course, unequal to it: Billy attacks Jud, at one point fending off retaliation by swinging the dead hawk at his mother and brother as they come for him. He escapes from the room and wanders the estate, wandering back too in memory to the time when his Dad had taken him to the pictures before they had returned home to find his mother embracing an 'uncle'. Billy's father had left and never come back; he, Billy, returns to the present – fatherless, hawkless, friendless, rootless, a potential delinquent who is still, in the real sense of the term, a 'little boy' – and goes back to the house that is not a home. The one thing that gave Billy's life a worthwhile focus has been taken from him; the capacity to love, to endow with dignity, to take pride in, all things which help to make emotional deprivations endurable, these are gone. The ending of the novel leaves no doubt as to the result: bitterness and frustration will ensue, the lot that of an estate boy from a sordid home, lacking guidance, fulfilment and, above all, understanding or encouragement from a society which is largely uncaring and motivated by selfish needs.

The film

The film is strongly recommended, but students of the book are advised not to confuse it with the film. Barry Hines worked on the screenplay with the director, Ken Loach, and the producer, Tony Garnett, but there can be no such thing as a faithful translation from book to screen; each operates in a different medium. Although some of the techniques used in *A Kestrel for a Knave* are cinematic (the flashback, for example), the differences between the visual and the printed are too various ever to be equated. There is, however, such a thing as loyalty to the spirit of a book, and this the film achieves outstandingly. In 'The Kes Dossier' (*Sight and Sound*, Summer 1970) John Russell Taylor gives an account of this small-budget film and the difficulties it met in getting to the wider public; there were, moreover, delays while it was held back from even limited distribution. It had a tight, eight-week shooting schedule, and was filmed entirely in Barnsley. The showing in the North broke all box office records and eventually it was shown at the Academy cinema in London, the London Film Festival of 1969 and at Cannes in 1970. The only (then) professional actor in *Kes* was Colin Welland, who played Mr Farthing. Many of the actors were local, and the inspired choice of the fifteen-year-old David Bradley as Billy Casper gave the film a wide appeal which, according to the viewing figures for its television showings, has not diminished. Just as the novel on which it is based is a modern classic. so, too, is the film a cinema classic and should be seen for its own particular merits: its fine visual qualities, its artistic coherence, its poignant realism.

Section summaries, critical commentaries, textual notes and revision questions

Since *Kes* is not divided into conventional chapters, the summaries and critical commentaries below are from sections of the novel where natural divisions fall.

Section 1: from 'There were no curtains up' to 'as his finger crept under the lines'. (pp.7–39).

Jud and Billy in bed, with Jud getting up to go to work. Later Billy gets up, makes a fire, tries to find something to eat and drink. He fails, realizes that Jud has taken his bike, and nearly arrives late for his newspaper round. Billy steals two bars of chocolate, and then sets off on the walk. From a milk dray he steals some orange juice and a carton of eggs. Having drunk the juice, he sets off again, reading the *Dandy* as he goes. Much later he returns to the shop, then goes home – children are now setting off for school – and sees his mother's boyfriend leaving the house. He argues with his mother (she wants some cigarettes), leaves the house, throws eggs on to the slates, and refuses to take a bet for Jud. When his mother has gone he goes to the shed and talks to the kestrel hawk, Kes.

There follows an immediate retrospect to the day when Billy first gets Kes. He steals some of Jud's snap – Jud returns to threaten him – and then calls for two of his friends. They are not up, so he sets off alone. He goes through the country fields and enters a wood. His first attempt on a nest finds it empty; then he watches a hawk return to its mate with its prey. Billy dozes but awakes to see the hawk again. He has a short argument with a farmer, but the latter shows him where the hawk's nest is. Billy is excited, and later goes to the library to try to get some books on the subject of hawks. Unable to take books out – he hasn't the requisite form signed by a parent – Billy goes to a bookshop and steals *A Falconer's Handbook*. Teased and bullied by Jud, watching his mother and Jud arguing, both intent on their coming Saturday evening pleasures, Billy is eventually left in peace to read his book.

Critical commentary

Note the simple but effective creation of early morning atmosphere at the opening of the novel. The short sentences reflect the cramped lives of Jud and Billy in the bed and, later, in their small world outside. Particular usages are drawn attention to in the notes below. The dialogue is natural, particularly recording the half-awake state of the speakers, the dialect unforced, obscene; the punch in the kidneys effectively establishes Jud's aggressively bullying nature which culminates in the destruction of the kestrel at the end of the novel. One of the threats constantly used by Jud is that Billy too will soon be working down the pit, another indication of their constricted lives. The shared clothes – Billy and Jud pick up what lies to hand – underline the deprived and sordid nature of their existence. Strangely, the lighting of the fire has a distinct method in it, perhaps preparing us for Billy's application in his training of the hawk. Note the realism of Billy scaling the wire fence and getting across the recreation ground, and the factual account which follows it, particularly the dialogue with Porter. There is some social comment in the fact that Billy is lucky to have the job in view of the competition for it.

Billy's stealing is his reflex way of surviving – after all, little or nothing is provided for him at home. His escape into the *Dandy* is a psychological reflex too, for his is a sordid world in which the ready visual humour of the comic comes as a welcome relief from the various degradations of survival. The visit to the prosperous house to deliver his paper is a pathetic incident, for Billy is looking into a cosy life of the kind which he will never know. In some ways, he will always be the outsider looking in. But Billy is remarkable for his resilience, and the incident in which he nearly brings down Porter is a briefly comic sequence. Arrived back home he is in the middle of sordid life again, with his mother's sluttishness, her intrigue with Reg, her debts at the local shop, the argument, the aggression, the escape; all the time we must remember that the central figure is *a child*, a child who has to assume grown-up stances in order to survive in this world. Again there is a certain comedy in the way he outwits his mother, and in his gesture in throwing the eggs. But there is also an ominous look forward in Billy's refusal to take Jud's betting instructions.

Billy's isolation is stressed by the fact of his talking to Kes. It is his only resource against a cruel world. The flashback takes us back to the day when he acquired Kes, and again we are aware of (a) the monotony of the arguments at home and (b) the sense of isolation again when his friends fail to join him on his early morning adventure. His attempts to rouse them are done with the usual vivid and factual description. As Billy makes for the country the description takes on a lyrical tone, almost as if the country and the woods are expressive of a natural beauty which is denied to the urban child. This is given in detail both from sound and sight, and we notice the inherent tenderness in Billy as he crouches over the thrush's nest and strokes the backs of the babies. The whole of this experience is felt, immediate, conveyed, with the tree-climbing incident indicative of Billy's determination and courage. Billy's reaction to the hawks is immediate, almost as if he has discovered something new about the quality of life, as indeed he has. Note the acute, minute observation of the writer as the hawk is described. The hostility of the farmer gradually decreases as he sees the genuine enthusiasm of the boy. We are aware that the pathos has not gone, for Billy responding to the hawk, wondering with inarticulate delight at its uniqueness, is still small, vulnerable, underprivileged, an urban mudlark outside the grown-up world. The library sequence is a study in non-communication, a child here treated as a child, the petty bureaucracy of rules a barrier between the boy and a genuinely sought aspect of education, the book about hawks. Billy shows his impetuosity in refusing to wait, while when he goes to the bookshop his natural thieving gets him the book he wants. There is a cinematic cut to Jud's reaction, the bent pages almost giving one the sense of wounding. The interaction with Jud and then with his mother shows Billy's distance from them and further underlines the pathos. Jud and Billy's mother are intent on the booze and sex of the evening to come; Billy is intent on returning to his book, yet his words to them, redolent of joy in the experience of the beauty of the hawk's movements, for example, show this boy as capable of a poetry beyond his sordid home conditioning. Jud's cheap use of the word 'bird' contrasts with Billy's true and excited one. Jud is vain without cause, Mrs Casper disorganized, late, and, and at the last moment, generous to cover her guilt, giving Billy money to get himself something to eat. This is a searing section of social and moral comment, the irony being that the boy who could so easily turn delinquent (his stealing shows his potential) finds a real interest which is unappreciated by his family, who are intent on their own sordid and wholly selfish pleasures.

Textual notes

In the following notes, no attempt is made to give every definition which can be found in a dictionary, although on occasions such definitions are given if they assist either the immediate sense or critical interpretation. Swear words and obscenities which have become commonplace both in print and in the visual media are likewise ignored.

Figurative language – for example, alliteration, metaphors and similes – are often referred to if they aid appreciation or develop a theme, but the keen student will find his own examples from the text which are not listed here. In the interest of time-saving, the page references preceding each entry are to the Penguin edition of *A Kestrel for a Knave* since this is the edition students are most likely to use. But since the notes are in the sequence of the book itself, they should be easily used by any student regardless of the edition.

Epigraph (facing p.7)
'An Eagle for an Emperor . . . a Kestrel for a Knave.' The title is ironic, since this epigraph to the novel traces the hunting birds suitable to be used by the highest and the lowest. Billy is the lowest, for in strict terms 'knave' originally meant 'boy', but it also means a rogue, a person of no principle, which would be the superficial view of Billy Casper anyway.

7 **There were no curtains up** The first sentence of the novel underlines the lack of ordinary domestic provision.

7 **Wind whipped the window** Unobtrusive alliterative effect which conveys the unprotected nature of the house and, by implication, of Billy.

7 **cough-coughed** The unhealthy closeness of the pair in the scantily covered bed is indicated.

7 **hutched** Covered.

7 Tha'd You'd.

8 drilled Made a small furrow.

8 thumped Billy in the kidneys This, of course, could be dangerous, and underlines the kind of life they lead – as well as showing Jud's capacity for violence.

8 Gi'o'er! Stop it!.

8 thi You.

8 thi sen Yourself.

8 thar up You're (already) up.

8 Hands off cocks; on socks Rhyming slang conveying the give and take of coarse sexual humour and at the same time the immediacy of life – the need to get up and go to work.

8 wafered Very thin. A fine descriptive word. Consider the size of the hand when compared with the thigh.

8 tha's to You had to.

9 his mother's sweater The sordidness of life further shown by the family's communal use of each other's garments.

9 like a bouquet of hydrangea flowers Ironic use of simile in view of the surroundings, hydrangeas being shrubs which have globular clusters of white, blue or pink flowers.

9 nog Small block.

9 bit i.e. into the wood.

9 tile i.e. on the hearth.

9 like the struts of a wigwam Like the supports of a Red Indian-style tent dwelling.

9 There were a packet of dried peas ... Notice that the sparse nature of the supplies in the pantry indicates the deprived, uncared-for state of Billy's life.

9 jamb Side post of doorway.

9 hiding some at nights i.e. concealing some food so that he's got something to eat in the mornings.

10 Well, of all the rotten tricks i.e. Jud has taken his bike.

10 pumps Light shoes, usually without fastening, originally worn for dancing.

10 dog-hole i.e. made by dogs in order to get through.

11 I nearly wa' though i.e. 'I was nearly (late)'.

11 squared off Brought the edges into an even line.

11 It's typical i.e. of your attitude.

12 They'll take your breath if you're not careful The fine ear of the author for a kind of sarcasm which is a commonplace of the area.

12 **owt** Anything.

12 **pebble-dash** Mortar with pebbles in it as coating for a wall.

12 **leaded** i.e. lead frames holding the glass.

12 **cropped verge** Closely-cut grassway, symbolizing the cared-for, superior nature of the neighbourhood.

13 NO HAWKERS No people carrying goods about in order to sell them. Ironically, a hawker is also a falconer.

13 **asphalt** Dark, bituminous pitch mixed with sand for surfacing roads, paths, etc.

13 **A thrush ran out...** This fine short passage merits the reader's close attention, since it carries a symbolic association. The thrush preys on the worm, Billy is forced to prey on anything he can; thrush eats worm, Billy eats stolen chocolate – an ironic parallel.

14 **Third class riding...** Again, the earthy, cliché humour.

14 **tab** The end of a cigarette.

14 **the flakes raged like a glass snow storm** Billy has made his drink a fizzy one. The reference is to the small ornaments which can be bought, particularly at seaside resorts, which show a winter scene behind glass or perspex. When they are shaken a simulated snow storm occurs.

14 **Toy traffic** Ironic sense of perspective underlining the idea of a small world.

14 **as clear as an ink blot** The comparison might well come from Billy's own consciousness in view of his troubled classroom experiences.

15 **the *Dandy*... *Desperate Dan*** The comic and its celebrated character, still in existence and going strong weekly. The story Billy reads, the escape into a world of fantasy, with predictable, obvious humour, carries its own irony. There is a knockabout flavour to the humour, for Dan is a desperate joker, whereas Billy is desperate in life. The whole paragraph, where the style exactly mirrors the drawings in the comic, should be closely examined by the reader. This is a small escape from reality into the ridiculous and grotesque; laughter, seeing another's misfortune (here the attendant's), often compensates for our own inadequacy.

16 **The hall and stairs were carpeted...** This description forms a poignant contrast to the 'home' where Billy lives.

16 **reminiscent of markings on a snake's back** Fine observation, and an image which perhaps signals the twists and turns and dangers of life.

16 **Evening** The now familiar, laboured sarcasm to imply that Billy has taken a long time.

16 **shotspread** Small lead pellets.

16 **grass in 'em** i.e. the fields. Billy means that he has done no harm by walking in them.

17 **learn you owt** Teach you anything.

17 **Ar, I'm bloody champion!** 'I feel fine'. Sarcasm again.

18 **a man appeared from round the side of the house** The implication is, of course, that he has spent the night with Billy's mother.

18 **capsule, like a bullet** The lipstick is being referred to, but there is a suggestion of killing, this early in the novel, in the short simile.

18 **mashed** Made.

19 **in t'book** Keep a record of it, allow (me) credit.

19 **a tanner** In pre-decimal terms a sixpence.

19 **like two pianists ready to begin** Ironic, since the projected performance of Billy and his mother is violent, not musical.

20 **feinted** Pretended, shammed.

20 **A skylark ... Higher and higher until it was just a song in the sky** Whether by unconscious or deliberate association, the author is echoing Shelley's famous *To a Skylark* (1820): 'Higher still and higher ... And singing still dost soar/And soaring ever singest.'

20 **crouching over them** There is a strong suggestion here of a bird protecting its young.

20 **parabola** The plane curve, the path (of the egg) under the action of gravity.

21 **laths** Thin strips of timber about an inch wide used for supports.

21 **Rufous brown** i.e. reddish-brown. But look closely at the description of the hawk – a superb example of stylistic economy, in which two lines only are required to delineate something of fearsome beauty.

21 **making her mouth ... Gooby** Billy is indicating contempt for his mother's verbal threats which she cannot carry out. Here, 'Gooby' is a misprint for 'Gobby', which means 'having too much to say for herself'.

21 **whooshed** The word is the sound, a simple, onomatopoeic effect being achieved.

21 **as clean as water** Simple simile to underline the essential goodness of what is natural.

22 **t'cage** The frame for hoisting and lowering men at the pit.

22 **stained leaves** i.e. already used, indicating a sloppy way of life, or perhaps even an enforced economy.

22 **before they'll set thi on** Before they'll give you a job.

22 **twat** Vulgar word for the female genitals, hence here a derogatory, abusive term.

22 **snap** Crisp, brittle cakes or biscuits, here probably meaning the food he will take down the pit.

23 **smattered** Hit (the panes) superficially, without damaging them.

23 **like a projection half-way down a waterfall** Again evidence of the author's almost casual observation of natural detail.

23 **tweezed** Fine if unusual verbal usage here to convey how one holds the lashes firmly apart.

23 **pinking** Sounding high-pitched, the word itself giving the onomatopoeic effect.

24 **round like the bulb of a thermometer** *A Kestrel for a Knave* is full of sudden images like this which reveal Hines's acute and associative powers of observation.

24 **snicket** Cut or alley.

24 **rashes of buttercups** Again the fine observation. They come up everywhere, like a rash on the skin.

24 **dog-daisies** Wild daisies, also known as ox-eye daisies.

24 **sorrel** An acid-leaved herb used in salads.

24 **underscored** Underlined, growing underneath.

24 **ubiquitous plantains** Low herbs, with broad flat leaves close to the ground, which were everywhere.

24–5 **A cushion of mist . . . climbing steadily like the finger of a clock** This is a fine poetic description, full of light, colour and what we have already come to regard as typically acute observation. It provides a poignant contrast with the sordid nature of Billy's day-to-day life. There is also a recognition in Billy himself, though it is unvoiced, of the ecstasy in nature which he is to find in the kestrel.

25 **as a barrage of shells** Not an inappropriate image, in view of the continuing noise and the immediacy.

25 **flushed a blackbird** Caused (the bird) to rise up and fly away.

25 **continuous relay** The sound is felt here, but the phrase echoes its movement in the air.

25–6 **a chaffinch gave out . . . flashing across the bars of the trees** The whole paragraph is a revelation of the author's sensitivity to the sights and sounds of nature.

26 **as snugly as a completed jig-saw** Another of the images which link nature and the simple, valued pleasures of family life.

26 **a riding** A green track (for riders) through or beside a wood.

26 **scots pine . . . whiskers** A reference to the Scotch fir, but the subtle

personification gives the tree a life and individuality of its own.

26 **stippling** The pattern in the bark.

26–7 **in segments like a caterpillar ... legs gripping and pushing** Not only is the natural description right, but this is one of the many references in the novel which underline the author's training in physical education.

27 **scrabbling** Scratching, groping about.

27 **planed off ... like a rabbit diving into its burrow** Frequently in this novel one aspect of nature is seen in terms of another.

27 **crackled like crisps ... like the dull red of a cooling poker glowing through the soot** Again the images are rich and immediate in sight and sound suggestions.

28 **sounding like one turn of a football rattle** Another fine sound effect with an unusual association.

28 **it held like a star** A fine, poetic moment. The hawk is, so to speak, the star in Billy's firmament, and at the very end, after the death of Kes, Billy sees, in the deserted picture palace, himself and Kes as 'stars'.

28 **primaries** The first feathers.

29 **lobbed off** Slowly, perhaps heavily, flew off.

29 **The man smiled ...** Technically, by side-footing the pebble he has scored a 'goal' – an instance of the fantasies we indulge in when we are walking along.

30 **and you'd be looking from six feet under** An ironic way of saying 'You'd kill yourself' (if you tried to climb up there).

30 **on an extender** i.e. an extending ladder.

31 **variegated complex** Irregular patches of colours bound together.

32 **lend** This is, of course, incorrect, but a commonplace misuse for 'borrow'.

34 **grate** Frame of metal bars in the road.

34 **Devotional** i.e. religious, to do with Divine worship.

34 *A Falconer's Handbook* A guide to the training of hawks for sport, with detail on the nature of rearing, etc.

34 **sparrow-hawk** A small hawk which preys on sparrows.

34 **arcade** Strictly speaking, a covered walk with shops along one or both sides.

35 **chuff me** 'To be chuffed' means to be very pleased. Here it merely indicates surprise.

35 **scuffled** Treated (the pages) roughly.

36 **a half-nelson** A wrestling-hold in which one arm is imprisoned behind the back by an opponent.

36 **wet** Silly.

36 **laterally** Raised sideways.

37 **I'll be laid watchin' a bird . . . she'll not have feathers** Jud's jealousy of Billy's new-found interest provokes a sexual coarseness of innuendo as seen here.

37 **flubbered** Puffed, distended.

38 **a double up** i.e. his bets (dependent on two horses winning) had been successful.

38 **treats you every night** i.e. pays for you (with the implication that it is in return for sleeping with him).

38 **fluffed the bob** Shook out, increased the effect of, the hair.

39 **florin** Pre-decimal coin worth two shillings.

39 **lip the words** i.e. shape their sounds. The implication may be that Billy is a slow reader, which would hardly be surprising.

Revision questions on Section 1

1 Write an account of Billy's home life as revealed in this section.

2 Explain in some detail how Billy comes to get the hawk.

3 In what ways does this section reveal that Billy is constantly in trouble, or likely to be in trouble? You should refer closely to the text in your answer.

4 Select seven or eight phrases from this section which illustrate Barry Hines's powers of description.

Section 2: from 'At the first sound of footsteps on the stairs . . .' to 'obliterated every other sound in the vicinity.' (pp.39–85).

Billy helps the drunken Jud to undress, gets him to bed, and hits him. He flees in momentary panic. He goes through the wood to the farmhouse and thence to the ruined wall, finds the nest and selects one of the young kestrels. He takes it home.

The story then cuts again to Billy answering his name in class and being reprimanded for his wit. There follows school assembly, with Gryce on the warpath, before Billy returns to the shed to feed Kes. His training of the bird is described, as well as its lashing out at a little boy who expresses a wish to stroke it. Then again we move into the present. Billy has fallen asleep in assembly and is publicly reprimanded by Gryce. He joins the other members of the 'smokers' union' for their caning, and arranges to fight MacDowall at break. Gryce lectures them, they empty their pockets, having first transferred the evidence to the messenger, who is innocent but found guilty. After the caning, Billy returns to Mr Farthing's lesson. This Fact and Fiction exercise contains Anderson's account of the tadpoles, and Billy is asked to tell a story about himself. Provoked and threatened, Billy gradually opens up into detail about the training of Kes. Mr Farthing cooperates over the technicalities, encouraging Billy to a full account. He explains how he 'flew her free'. After the facts comes the fiction – 'A Tall Story' and Billy writes one about how he would like his home life to be.

At break Billy is provoked by insults into a fight with Mac-Dowall. Mr Farthing breaks up the encounter, and is severe on MacDowall, the bully. He is sympathetic to Billy. Billy talks of his life and teachers as they are, and of how he is picked on despite the fact that he has reformed and is interested only in Kes. Mr Farthing asks if he can see Billy with the bird.

Commentary

The section opens with the sordid reality of Jud's drunkenness, which has something of a comic element too. Billy's chanting has something of the daredevil in it, though he knows that he is safe, since Jud is incapable of responding. The bravado culminates in the blow. Fine and economical description accompanies Billy's trip to find the nest, and we notice that there is considerable excitement generated in the account, almost as if the boy in his obsession realizes that he is on the edge of finding something worthwhile, something that will change his life, as indeed it does. The contact with the owl has a moving element of reassurance in it; Billy is not alone, as he is in life. The single-word effects in the style show how careful and slow are Billy's movements towards the nest. There is also a very considered use of words which register the facts of that movement, together with the author's descriptive appraisal of it. There is an element of tenderness in

Billy's selection of the young hawk and his care for each of the others.

We now move back into time present. The 'German Bight' joke shows Billy as outsider again, his imagination private and alive to his own experiences. Again there is the sense of pathetic isolation, and this is here linked to the hostility (because he is 'crackers') of his classmates. The teacher's jibe is a cheap one. Notice the authentic atmosphere of the school assembly, with the coughing and hawking noises providing Gryce with that standby of the schoolmaster, the sarcasm which is vainglorious and often leads to injustice, here the punishment of the hapless MacDowall – ironic justice in view of the bullying capacity of that boy. The chosen hymn carries its irony, since it is manifestly at variance with the experience of the boys who are compelled to sing it. The threat to make them sing, the reference to the slaughterhouse, are far removed from the essence of Christianity which are contained in the words. The reading is a mockery of religion, and we feel that we are present at an imposed ritual that has nothing to do with faith or, more important, the practice of that faith.

Billy's training of Kes is done in superb detail, convincing, immediate, the mark of his ability to absorb training, take a pride in it. He has educated himself here, a marked contrast with the failure of formal education to make any impression on him except as victim. There is also a tenderness in his action, a giving of love and a receiving of love – in the bird's obedience and its return to him – which he is lacking in his home life. The word 'gently' is the key word here. His reflex humour is somewhat more sadistic, as is revealed in his exchanges with the inquisitive little boy. The hawk's response to the latter provides a vivid moment of excitement, almost of fear. Again we return with hard immediacy to the present, with Billy caught sleeping in assembly, a pathetic reaction as a result of his overworked life outside school. Gryce's injustice is again demonstrated when he says what he *thought* Billy was doing. The incident with the paper is humorous, that with the messenger unpleasant, the bullying and threats perhaps a mirror of the society in which the boys live, where the criminals degrade the innocent and the weak. Gryce's lecture is interrupted by his contemplation of the outside which 'hinted of Spring', the irony being that there is no spring in the drab lives before him. His failure to understand – in some ways his lecturing of the smokers' union is a parody of such commonplace schoolmasterly practice – spells out the nature of the generation gap. It is full of pathos, and is in effect a comment on our way of life and the nature of our society. There is a hopelessness about it all which is moving, for Gryce knows what we all know, that the use of the cane will make no difference.

The Fact and Fiction sequence reflects good imaginative teaching. It also shows Mr Farthing as someone who is interested in the boys and who does not score off them cheaply. Not only is the tadpole incident amusing, it is also an indication of Mr Farthing's sympathetic personality, since the boy feels confident and relaxed enough to tell the story, as does Billy after him. Though Farthing forces him to do some work and accuses him of sleeping, he doesn't punish him in the accepted sense of the word – accepted sense for the boys – but succeeds in drawing out of him something that he really cares about in a life which has little for him. This is both good teaching and humane practice, though he makes the mistake of giving the class bait for mocking Billy when he refers to the 'stuffed one'. He redresses this by thoughtfully waiting for Billy to collect himself.

Notice the technique of Mr Farthing's questions. They help to promote fluency in Billy as he warms to the subject which finds him always warm. Succeeding questions do not break the fluency, but ensure that definitions are given – jesses, bating – which will help the understanding, and hence the interest, of the rest of the class. This is not education in a vacuum, but practical education, and Billy moves from defensive clown to centre-stage. Mr Farthing shows that he has the boys' education always at the forefront of his mind by writing important words on the board, and he has the tact and persuasiveness to prevent Billy from becoming self-conscious. The subtlety of the author is apparent throughout Billy's story, for the way in which Billy trains Kes is being cleverly duplicated by Mr Farthing, who is subtly encouraging or training Billy in full self-expression. The terrible irony is that Billy, unlike the hawk he describes, will never be allowed to fly free in a society which is training him for nothing. That free flying is the climax of Billy's account. These facts contrast pathetically with Billy's tall story to come.

That story is one of the finest things in the novel. If the spelling reflects the failure of conventional and rote-learning education, then there is great compensation in the expression which reveals the inner heart of the child. The note below gives its salient features, but see also how Billy uses part of his experience – the visit to the large and prosperous house on his paper-round – to fill in details of how he would like life to be. It is expressive of his need for love – at home and at school – and the attendant pathos, which the reader is fully aware of – is that he will never get either, except from someone as rare and understanding as Mr Farthing.

Barry Hines is adept at contrast, and after this outpouring on paper – and writing is certainly one remove from reality – he gives us that reality in all its immediate and frightening rawness. MacDowall is intent on provocation, the mark of the obvious, used-to-getting-his-own-way bully. The sexual innuendo about Billy's mother and Jud's illegitimacy is calculated to elicit the unbalanced response from Billy. The dialogue is as crudely humorous as one would expect from these deprived estate boys who, of course, know everybody else's business. That knowledge is the product of their idleness, and when Farthing arrives to sort things out he uses the same threats to MacDowall – the big bully who will be beaten up by the bigger bully syndrome – since he knows that is the only language – and morality – that Mac-Dowall has been conditioned to understand. Before that there is the graphic account of the beginning of the fight, with a particular focus on the dustbin-climbing spectators. There is also the humorous aside of the little fights beginning on the outskirts of the main one as 'sideshows'. Not only is Farthing a good teacher, he is also a good disciplinarian, and once more displays his humanity when he takes the trouble to probe Billy's individual case. In mentioning the punishment of the messenger Billy reveals that he has a moral core, hidden though it may be by tears, dirt, impertinence and reflex stealing. Even in this adversity Billy has spirit enough to impersonate teachers. Through Billy the author enunciates the lack of teaching concern for the lower-level ability range. It is a genuine comment on the limitations of an educational system which has teachers catering for the high flyers but doing little to interest those who are less able, and having little time for their interests anyway.

Billy also indicates another moral area of his life, the difficulty of becoming moral when you have been known for not being so. He rightly gives this as the reason for MacDowall's picking on him. Billy continues to explain why he is a victim, but he also makes some reasonable comments on the way he and his kind go with gangs, steal, waste time because there is nothing for them to do. They are conditioned among themselves to be anti-establishment, hence their rejection of youth clubs. Billy reveals his dislike of games, the meaninglessness of any work he will go to when he leaves school; Farthing counters with genuine interest in the boy and asks if he may see the hawk.

39 **re-adjusting his feet** Trying to appear as if not drunk, though he obviously is.

40 **like a man in fetters** An appropriate simile. He is the prisoner of drink.

40 **pish** Drunk.

40 **a blind smile** Completely pictures his unseeing state, in a sense 'blind' drunk.

41 **a still** The author has an eye for graphic immediacy. A 'still' is a photograph used to advertise a film by showing one moment of its action. Here the crucial moment is 'held' by the writer. It suspends the action, and indicates the importance of that moment.

42 **it formed a curtain . . .** A natural one, poetically and sympathetically seen.

42 **formed pillars and lintels, terraced doorways** A further underlining of the suggestion that the wood is a much more real home than the one from which Billy has just escaped.

42 **maintained contact with the owl** A sympathetic underlining of Billy's natural affinity with nature (later it is seen on another level by his care for the dog that strays on to the football pitch). This is positive communication as distinct from the non-communication of speech between Billy on the one hand and Jud, or his mother, on the other; these last two are non-listeners too, intent on their own forthcoming pleasures.

42 **jut** Projection, sticking out.

43 **crabbing . . . back-tracking** Moving sideways, then turning back again (to explore).

43 **belly-flop** i.e. flat on his stomach.

43 **eyas kestrel** A young hawk taken from its nest for training.

43 **clucked down** Pushed deeply.

44–5 *Fisher . . . German Bight . . . Cromarty* Billy is right about the shipping forecast on radio. These are North Sea areas, the last being off the Scottish coast, while German Bight and Fisher cover the area from the German coastline to the tip of Scandinavia.

45 raked . . . killing the sound The comparison reminds one of machine-gun fire – and the verbal equivalent of that can be killing.

45 pearls of wisdom Heavy sarcasm, already indulged in at Billy's expense.

45 vertical like a fishing float i.e. as it is on the surface of the water.

45 lolloped Moved in an ungainly way.

46 gouged a miscoloured egg, the focal point of the whole grid Heavy circling of the absence mark, with the 'grid' being the register.

46 bloomed white An image from nature to underline what is unnatural or imposed.

46 lectern Reading or singing desk.

46 swishsmack Onomatopoeic coinage of the author's which effectively conveys the sound.

46 like a bulldog up on its hind legs The simile has a deliberately comic overtone, a caricature or parody of what is real – it is not dissimilar from the comic-grotesque of the *Dandy*.

46 revving Sarcasm again, throat clearings being compared to the repetitious noise of a car engine.

46 like the vibrations of a tuning fork The latter is a two-pronged steel fork designed to give a particular note (especially middle C) when struck.

46 skittering Moving lightly, rapidly.

47 Re-stored to life, and power, and thought The words of the hymn carry their own irony in the context – the non-education most of the boys are receiving.

47 dirge Song sung at a burial or in commemoration of the dead. A lament.

48 drapes Curtains.

48 Never despise one of these little ones . . . The whole passage has a poignant and ironic reference to Billy, who strays and is not saved, but the monotony of the reading – unaware, mechanical – underlines the payment of lipservice to a religion that is rendered meaningless to so many and is so often not applied to those who are in most need of it.

48 dried mutes The deposits, droppings.

49 crozzled Shrivelled, burned up.

49 gauntlet An armoured, protective glove.

49 **like someone up on the top board for the first time** Another of the many images from sport – here from diving.

49 **a swivel . . . jesses** The first is the ring and pivot which serves as a connection between two parts and enables one to revolve without the other; the second, the straps of silk or leather round the legs of the hawk.

49 **snagged** Caught, become attached.

49 **bated** Flew off the glove.

50 **jonked** Onomatopoeic as the wheels pass over a different surface.

50 **It's a piece o'leg off a kid it caught yesterday . . .** Billy has a sadistic sense of humour, perhaps as a result of his tough upbringing.

51 **straddling** Standing across, legs wide apart.

51 **mantled** Concealed, covered.

51 **cul-de-sac** Blind alley, street with one entrance which is also the only exit.

51 **as quick as a house of cards** The comparison is apt, since they are vulnerable, easily knocked over, as, indeed, is Billy.

53 **smokers' union** The now familiar heavy sarcasm.

53 **pay their dues** A continuation of the above 'joke', though their 'subscriptions' will consist of the cane.

53 **foyer** Large room or space in which people can move freely.

54 **Gryce pudding** A fairly obvious punning (rice) name for the Headmaster.

55 **The lawn stretching down . . . the only clean feature of the whole picture** A fine symbolic commentary on the wintry scene outside which corresponds to the wintry scene inside – the delinquent boys – which Gryce is contemplating.

55 **there's something happening today that's frightening** This refers directly to one of the major themes of the novel, the failure both of education and of society in their dealings with the young who have no direction in which to go.

56 **just a sheen with nothing worthwhile or solid underneath** This might be compared with the description of the silver birch through the windows; it has both sheen and solidity, and this indicates the permanence of nature.

56 **all-things-bright-and-splendiferous age** A conscious parody, with ironic overtones, of the hymn which begins 'All things bright and beautiful'.

56 **fodder for the mass media** i.e. providing material for the newspapers and television to talk about and show.

57 **ladened up** Filled.

57 like the warming bar of an electric fire . . . cooled to the colour of dripping A vivid contrast of the man-made and the natural, meaningfully registering the extremes of reaction in the boy.

57 broddling Probing, poking.

57 like a prioll of Jacks Three jacks in a hand of playing cards.

58 ruttled up into soft cushions i.e. soft flesh with grooves in between.

58 Except for the messenger . . . The caning of this boy symbolizes injustice, hard usage in a hard world.

58 perched side-saddle i.e. sitting on the desk, but with both legs on the same side.

59 rode it Suffered it with tolerance.

60 flitted Departed, moved away.

61 spook Ghost.

61 roaring Crying loudly.

61 The class up to their knees in tadpoles This device, involving the class in the *facts* of the story, has a Dickensian tone about it.

61 a pause for assimilation i.e. time allowed to take the *facts* in.

61 to inspire an emulator To get an account of an experience which would be even better.

63 'Else tha dies 'If you don't tell the story, you'll die'.

64 It must have tumbled from a nest Even here, Billy reverts to the reflex lie. We know that he deliberately took it.

64 I suppose I must be in select company Even Mr Farthing indulges in a little sarcasm at times!

64 through their stomachs i.e. through their appetite for food.

65 t'shaft The rib of feather.

65 keen Hungry, eager.

65 jesses See note p.27.

66 Then you get your swivel Note the meticulous detail, the actual mastery of sequence, in Billy's account; his interest captured, he has 'educated' himself to do things properly.

68 You just couldn't reckon it up at all You could never be certain (of how the hawk would react).

68 missen Myself.

68 t'smack Exactly.

68 sharp set Hungry.

69 she came like a rocket Just the kind of image – from space exploration, or local fireworks – which Billy would use.

69 **she's forced to go** i.e. though he is hoping against hope that the hawk will fly directly to him for the meat.

69 **t'lure** The apparatus used for recalling the hawk – often feathers within which there is food, taken by the hawk, which is held by a thong.

69 **a bolus** Here, a misprint for *bolas*, a South American missile of two or more balls tied by a length of cord. It is used by cowboys for bringing down cattle. They throw the bolas, which wraps round the cattle's legs.

69 **The donkey and the carrot principle** i.e. holding the carrot before the donkey's nose in order to make it move forward, and keeping it moving by repeating this.

70 **enter 'em at game** i.e. fly them at their prey, e.g. goose, rabbits, etc.

70 **It's a right pantomime** This is Billy's way of expressing the humour of the experience.

70 **peregrinations** Here it means the mental journeys (being taken by the class) to find the answer.

71 **Blimey** An expression of surprise (God blind me).

71 **'A Tall Story'** After what has gone before – the stimulating accounts of Anderson and Billy – this 'essay' title is lacking in inspiration, the schoolmaster's fall back to a stereotyped subject, though his illustration of it (p.72) is quite amusing.

72 **appended** Added.

73 **One day I woke up ... and then we went to bed** Billy's 'tall story' is a poignant revelation of what he would like from life – and what he feels is impossible that he should ever have – the return of his father, Jud's departure (permanent), his mother staying at home and doing the cooking, visits to the pictures, ice-cream, recurring fish and chips. In the psychological sense it is the most important paragraph in the novel, showing that the basic needs of childhood (much more important than formal education) like love, security, happiness, are singularly absent from Billy's life. Ironically, one is aware at the same time of the kind of 'mark' Billy might be expected to receive for this misspelt, largely unpunctuated piece of wish-fulfilment.

75 **cock o' t'estate** The best, strongest fighter; in modern brief graffiti terms, 'Jud Rules OK'.

75 **right brother** The implication is that Jud (or Billy) is illegitimate.

76 **before I spit on thi an' drown thi** Typical teasing, bullying humour, calculated to antagonize. It stresses Billy's smallness, too.

76 **moulded into shifting waves under the weight** But the hardness of the coke forms a natural contrast within the simile, and makes it effectively, physically felt.

76 **linear form** i.e. in lines.

77 **like a row of dominoes** Simple simile, very effective because it would be within the experience of the watchers. Dominoes is still played, often in pubs.

77 **their heads outlining a rough spotlight . . . the beam** The association is with the theatre or an open-air boxing ring, the 'entertainment' image being extended by mention of 'sideshows to the main attraction'.

77 **like a terrier shakes a rat** Note the appropriateness of the simile to MacDowall, who is only 'big' in relation to Billy.

78 **cokey beach** Throughout this and other sections there are references, which have a pathetic overtone, to the real seaside, which many of these boys would never have seen.

78 **boyo** Boy, but with the implication here perhaps of being a braggart or bully.

79 **like partners learning to dance** A certain clumsiness, ironic emphasis in this grotesque picture.

82 **They're not bothered about us** Barry Hines is underlining the fact that the less able are not catered for in the present educational system.

82 **cretins** Deformed idiots, here a term of abuse.

84 **a goshawk** A large, short-winged hawk.

84 **purgatory** A place of spiritual purging and cleansing, here meaning 'Hell'.

85 **to twirl his whistle . . . suspended from one forefinger** For a moment Mr Farthing, caught up in the art of training the kestrel in his mind, almost mimes that art!

Revision questions on section 2

1 Show how the author successfully mingles past and present in this section.

2 Write an account of the school assembly. In what ways would you say that it is true to life?

3 Write an essay on the role of Mr Farthing in this section.

4 Explain, in some detail, the process of training a hawk. You may quote in support of your answer.

5 Write an essay on what you consider to be the most dramatic incident in this section.

6 By close reference to the text, show how the author makes things vivid by his use of metaphors and similes.

Section 3: from 'The toilets were empty' to 'and the damp seeped through the light grey flannel, staining it charcoal.' (pp.85–108).

Description of the toilets, factual, with some expressive comparisons, and Billy alone, washing his hands and indulging in a pantomime of making bubbles. In the changing-room the master, Mr Sugden, mocks Billy for having no kit, and then gives him a ridiculously large pair of shorts to wear. They make for the field, Mr Sugden eventually picking Billy, who dislikes football, for his team. Sugden has his Manchester United shirt on, makes Billy play in goal, and commentates on the game and the imaginary teams as well as refereeing and playing. The match proceeds, with Billy letting in a goal at one end and Sugden as referee awarding himself a penalty from which he scores at the other. Billy does some acrobatics and balancing on the cross-bar, and then proceeds to demonstrate his way with animals as he pets a dog which has come on and disturbed the game. After removing the dog he watches the boys come out of school in the distance, and is reprimanded by Sugden for not having changed his dinner sitting. The football match becomes progressively more serious, and eventually Billy lets in the winning goal. Later Sugden slaps h n for not having a shower. He forces him to have one, with the water temperatures varied, and has three guards to prevent Billy from getting out. When he does emerge, Billy is forced to dry himself on his shorts.

Commentary

When Billy is alone, as here washing his hands and making bubbles, he is at his happiest, and is even imaginative. Note the insufferable vanity of Sugden, who plays out with the boys his own fantasy about himself as a famous footballer (variously identified) but also enjoys taking it out on Billy. He is to be contrasted with Mr Farthing, and compared with the boy Mac-Dowall as a bully. Instead of explaining the word 'Stimulating' to Billy he enjoys playing on the boy's ignorance, thus demonstrating that he, Sugden, is not really interested in education. His 'whipped-dog whining impersonation' is much more degrading to him than it is to Billy; we are aware that Sugden always calls the tune, and that he is prepared to cheat physically and verbally to get his own way and to stimulate his own vainglorious belief in himself. Note also the pathos of Billy's small earnings being already spoken for, and the sadistic pleasure that Sugden gets from hitting Billy with the ball and swatting him later. All these things emphasize that Billy is a victim. There is further sadism in the ridiculous choice of the shorts, for Billy's attempts to get them on cause general laughter, with Billy as the focus once more. When Billy says that he is shouting to keep warm this is physically true. The selection of the teams has an element of farce in it, and also an element of cruelty, since those who are left until last are manifestly the ones who are not wanted or who are very poor anyway. There is a splendidly ironic sense of contrast between the football gear of Mr Sugden, even down to the elaborate tying of the bandages, and the miscellaneous shorts/shirts/non-accessories of the boys; in brief, it is a contrast between vanity and ability as well as between middle-class affluence and poverty. A further area of humour is seen in Sugden's affectations, whether they be assuming the identity of a footballer or acting as commentator/referee who really has all the say all the time.

I have said that the game is a rich comic sequence (see below). It is really farce, but farce taken seriously by Sugden, as seriously as if it were a real game. And this is where the real humour lies, but there is an element of blackness in it. Sugden may be a figure of fun, but he is dangerous. His kicking the ball at Billy after the first goal is a foretaste of the sadistic torture of the showers which is to come. The focus on Billy after this reflects his poverty, since the shirt he is wearing has to be used for the game and for everyday wear. The interaction between the boys and Sugden as the game goes on is both funny and serious; the boys recognize Sugden's ineptitude, short temper and vanity only too well. There is also the simple comedy of his lack of physical fitness. Billy as lion and chimpanzee is expressive of his contempt for the game, and he undermines that game by his imagination and resourcefulness, since all the boys stop to look at him performing. The dog gives Billy the opportunity to display his real talent, a talent that has no measure in the educational scale. His dealing with the dog shows compassion and humanity as distinct from the incompetence of the majority of the boys and Sugden's totally impractical suggestion. Billy is sharp enough to see that the dog may be his means of escape from the wretched game. He displays quite a bit of humour about his own situation, with his bones supposedly broken in one foot and frostbite in the other, as he puts it. Billy uses his imagination in focusing on the 'midgets', and the importance of Kes is seen in his determination to feed the hawk at lunchtime. Vivid description characterizes the perspective that Billy maintains on pedestrians and cars before he is called back into the strife of the game. The pinball-machine image is drawn from the life experience of most of the boys and is therefore particularly appropriate, and notice the distinct colour effects, as in a film. There is a fine balance struck between Billy's wish to end the game so that he can go, and Sugden's determination to win. This struggle is the central focus, and the whole of the shower incident is Sugden's revenge for the denting of his own image by the defeat which, to be fair, Billy has done his best to bring about. The power of Sugden and his exercise of it is frightening in its intensity; it looks beyond the showers to the concentration camps, a living and vivid example of man's inhumanity to child. The water torture, the hired bullies, push things to a climax, but Billy's sudden reappearance lowers the physical and emotional temperature, ensures an anti-climax of laughter and, for Sugden, a deep frustration.

85 **Like a bag of cream puffs . . .** Almost the kind of image in which the boys might think.

86 **smiled like the Bisto Kid** A famous advertisement on hoardings in the 1920s and 1930s representing a ragged boy with a seraphic smile on his face as he smells the aroma of Bisto – a gravy. He is accompanied by his equally ragged sister. The advertisement appeared again on hoardings and later, on television. The association with Billy is obvious.

86 **the membrane** Connective tissue.

86 **oblivion** End, finish.

86 **Then out it came, a jewel . . . the buff of air . . . lathered palm** The whole sequence is allegorical – the bubble, like the dream of wish-fulfilment, is burst by reality, just as Billy's happiness – the hawk – is to be destroyed by Jud's revenge.

87 **nipped the slit as firmly as a row of surgical stitches** A fine image to indicate method, neatness – and it also serves as a contrast to the games kit of the boys.

88 **as though he was murdering him with a boulder** An ominous comparison. Sugden later does his best to 'murder' Billy's spirit.

89 **like a brave little clown** A fine image – this is what Billy is forced to be.

90 **goosey arms** i.e. having goose-pimples through the cold.

91 **a hare-lip** A split in the upper lip.

91 **a crew-cut** i.e. hair cut short all over.

91 **Hobson's choice** The option of taking the one thing offered or nothing. It is derived from the name of a Cambridge carrier, Tobias Hobson, who let out horses, and is said to have compelled customers to take the horse which happened to be next to the stable door, or go without.

92 **like a plum pudding on the tray of his hand** This image makes a caricature, a cartoon, of Sugden.

92 **Liverpool ... Manchester United** First Division soccer sides of considerable reputation and achievement both in English and European football.

92 **Bobby Charlton ... Denis Law** The first, who played for Manchester United throughout his career, scored more goals for England than any other player; the second an outstanding Scottish international of many years' standing who also played for Manchester United.

93 **Law's in the wash this week** Mr Sugden means, of course, the shirt which has the same number as that worn by Law. The irony is that there is no self-mockery in the statement; Sugden preens himself throughout on his knowledge and ability, but the first is questionable and the second is non-existent.

93 **the portal leading into the gladiatorial arena** Heavy irony. Gladiators fought at the arena in Rome, being a major part of the entertainment. 'Portals' is a high-flown word for 'gateway'

93–4 **And both teams are lined up ... Manchester United versus ...** Sugden wishes, of course, to play two roles here, player and commentator, and obviously thinks it is his function to create 'atmosphere' in this way.

94 **Spurs** Tottenham Hotspur, a famous North London football club.

94 **cudgel it upfield in a travesty of a dribble** This emphasizes the lack of ball ability, the clumsiness of Sugden. It makes him a humorous, grotesque figure.

95 **for a whippet perhaps** The boy's only defence is to answer criticism

with sarcasm. A whippet is a cross-bred of the greyhound type, used
for racing.

95 **scissor-jumped** i.e. spreading his legs apart, but bringing them
sharply together again.

95 **giant-striding** In view of his size – and what he is wearing – this
emphasizes Billy's self-imposed role of a clown.

95 **when Billy saw the stare of his eyes** Mr Sugden is going to be
revenged – Billy has let in a goal – by kicking the ball hard at him. Billy
sees his intention.

96 **a chuffing carthorse** He's slow and cumbersome, 'chuffing' being a
substitute for a stronger, abusive word.

97 **the referee awarded them a penalty** Note the irony. Sugden is
referee-biased – and, of course, penalty-taker. This football match is a
rich sequence, a humorous account of a big man behaving like a little
boy and sadistically taking it out on those who undermine his image of
himself as a great games-player.

97 **growling like a little lion . . . Field Crescent** This is a fine
paragraph. Billy's make-believe has an uncomfortable reality about it.
The boys are kept in for safety; but what happens when they escape?

97 **and make you red hot** A typical Sugden remark, implying use of the
cane.

98 **yarring** This word reflects the sound of their shouts.

98 **'Mr Wolf'** A children's game in which one child plays the part of the
wolf but, by a process of question and movement, makes another child
replace him.

99 **I'd sooner take meat away from a starving lion** There are strong
associations between the dog and Billy – both are strays in a sense – but
the remark underlines Sugden's cowardice.

100 **One to make and the match to win** A fine piece of irony, an echo
from the other end of the social scale, the public school cricket match.
The echo is from Henry Newbolt's *Vitae Lampada*:

> 'Ten to make and the match to win –
> A bumping pitch and a blinding light,
> An hour to play and the last man in . . .
> 'Play up! play up! and play the game!'

This last line is the refrain in every verse.

100 **pulling a sucked lemon face** i.e. hollowing his cheeks.

100 **stork fashion** On one leg.

100 **A young midget walked from behind the nail** Fine sense of
perspective – notice the activity of Billy's imagination, further
evidence of his capacity for experience and appreciation.

101 **You look as if you've had Thalidomide** This indicates Sugden's

needlessly cruel nature. The drug Thalidomide, prescribed as a soothing draught for pregnant women, caused them to produce malformed babies. The drug was withdrawn, and after a court case lasting for some years compensation was paid by the drug firm to the children and their parents.

101 **hawser** Cable, rope.

102 **drayhorse** Large, powerful horse used for drawing a brewer's cart.

102 **a sausage . . . a dumpling** Perhaps a conscious anticipation of the school dinner he is missing.

103 **Stalemate** In chess, a draw. Here it means deadlock, each waiting for the other to make a move.

104 **gurgle at the grate** i.e. of water.

104 **Eros-like** Greek god of love, a reference to the statue of Eros in Piccadilly Circus.

104 **a-jiggle** Rocking, jerking lightly.

104 **refractions** Deflections of light at angles.

105 **chassé** A gliding step in dancing.

105 **pigmentation of his skin** The natural colouring matter.

105 **flexion of the knee** Bending, curve.

105 **frown-like furrows** i.e. creases, as in the brow of a worried or thoughtful person.

105 **a sabre of shadow** i.e. a curve of shadow (like the blade of a sabre).

107 **guards** Ominous and loaded use of the word, outlining the menacing, bullying capacity of Sugden.

107 **snapping** Onomatopoeic usage, which has the movement and sound of the vowels.

107 **mesmeric beat** Rhythmic hypnosis, 'mesmeric' being derived from the Austrian physician, F. A. Mesmer, who died in 1815.

108 **as though Punch had appeared above them hugging his giant cosh** The reference is to the grotesque, hump-backed and curved-nose figure of the traditional Punch and Judy show.

108 **planed the standing droplets** i.e. using his hands like a tool which smoothes the surface.

108 **ruttled** Here it appears to mean 'stuck in grooves'.

Revision questions on Section 3

1 Write an account of the football match, bringing out clearly the nature of the comedy.

2 In what ways does Billy reveal his imagination while the game is going on?

3 Write an account of any two incidents which you have particularly enjoyed in this section.

4 Write down in some detail what it is about this section that makes you feel uneasy.

Section 4: from 'Home, straight home' to the end of the novel (pp.108–160).

Billy goes home, takes a gun, trains it on various articles; after this he picks up Jud's betting slip and the money. From the garage he kills a sparrow, then gets Kes out, frees her, but is interrupted by Mr Farthing. The latter watches as Billy maintains control of the lure and of the bird. After she takes the lure, Billy presents her with the dead sparrow. Afterwards he goes to the shed with Mr Farthing, tells him about the other birds he has kept, and finds that he and the teacher share an admiration for the unique qualities of Kes. After Mr Farthing has left Billy goes to the betting shop, but does not place Jud's bet; he leaves and buys fish and chips instead, then goes to the butcher's for a quarter of a pound of beef. He also buys cigarettes and eats his dinner on the way back to school.

In class that afternoon Billy sees Jud through the window. He keeps close to a teacher when the classes change over, and manages to elude Jud by dodging through the school. He hides in the boiler room, dozes off, comes back into school, and finds that he has missed his Youth Employment interview. Now he waits for it outside the medical room. During the interview he is fidgety and incapable of concentration. Once outside, he runs home, goes to the shed, and finds that Kes is gone. He searches for Jud, then goes out into the field swinging the lure for Kes to come. It is all in vain. He goes to the betting shop, learns of Jud's anger, and careers through fields and woods in his desperate search for Kes. He returns home, questions Jud, whose temper is frayed anyway. Billy tries to get comfort for Jud's destruction of the hawk from his mother, but she pushes him away. Billy recovers the dead Kes from the bin, asks his mother to punish Jud, and then attacks Jud himself. Billy runs away. He wanders

the estate and then enters a derelict cinema which he remembers
going to with his father. He triumphs in imagination with Kes.
He goes home, and buries the bird.

Commentary

The garage is described in meticulous factual detail. Billy's devo-
tion to Kes is shown by the fact that he is prepared to kill for her,
hence the shooting of the sparrow. But before that there is the
indoor practice, with the focus on the coins which Billy is to
spend on himself and Kes, Jud's bet which will bring down the
wrath of his half-brother on him. Notice always the intense
realism of the account, which makes every action, whether reflex
or violent, present to us in visual detail – again like a film. The
names of the horses are significant, for Billy is often spoken of as
a crackpot and the hawk is to die, though Jud of course does not
deign to tell Billy that Kes is dead.

The shooting of the sparrow is also cinematic, the rifle as
camera being used to good effect, but there is an ominous look
forward too; the death of the sparrow is as anonymous, in one
sense, as the coming death of Kes. Again the training process,
with its patience and repetition, is described, and the sentences
are cunningly structured, fashioned to approximate to the
swoop and then the rising flight of the hawk. In other words, the
style fits the subject. It is an exciting sequence. In the course of
discussion with Mr Farthing Billy reveals how much he has
learnt about the behaviour of Kes by trial and error. The
devouring of the sparrow has a deliberate realism about it; no
detail is spared for the squeamish. The following description is
particularly vivid, the intestines coming out 'like a watch on a
chain'. The destruction of the sparrow is as complete as the
destruction of Kes is to be later. Notice how clean the shed is, a
tribute to Billy's application and care, and notice also the reference to his other pets, which provided what love there has been
in his life. The discussion of the hawk's contours almost becomes
artistic, and the key phrase which defines the uniqueness is 'a
pocket of silence'. The fact that both Mr Farthing and Billy are
talking low further emphasizes the quality of the hawk. Billy's
fierceness over the fact that Kes is not a pet shows the real – and
almost adult – pride that he takes in her, and makes the coming

tragedy all the more horrific. It is casually accentuated, after Mr Farthing has gone, by Billy taking the minute skull and bones.

The betting shop sequence has the now familiar sordid realism, and in deciding whether to place the bet or not Billy is himself gambling, a terrible irony being that he loses all that he values by doing so. And even then his own gambling urges him that he should take the bet. Billy is moved by hunger and Kes's needs, and succumbs to temptation. Before that he has cross-questioned the man about the horses' chances, gambling here again by hoping that they will not win. When he gets to the fish and chip shop we are reminded of his smallness. When he buys cigarettes we feel again that he is trying to conform to the code of his classmates like MacDowall.

In the afternoon we feel the menace of Jud once Billy looks out of the window and sees him. Again there is an edge of excitement about the narrative, and the cinematic effect of the appearance of Jud's upper body coming into view creates a mounting fear in Billy's mind. The colour, or rather lack of it, the tears, the bell, are all expressive of mounting tension. His sticking close to the teacher is a survival exercise, while his flight into the toilets is evocative of panic. The kicking of the cubicle doors has the impact of pistol shots, the piling of the coats almost the reflex action of an animal hiding in its nest. Short sentences and single words maintain the menacing atmosphere, and every time the boy stops or hides we get his perspective, a kind of Billy's eye view of everything. The descent into the boiler-house has a claustrophobic quality. All the time the reader feels, such is the pace of the narrative and the pace of Billy's flight, that no matter what he does there is no escape. Sleep of course is a temporary refuge, and the clichés which describe Billy in the warmth of the boiler-house reflect this.

The continued tension is seen in Billy's initial attempts to open the door, and once outside the short, sharp sentences convey the speed of his movement, while 'quickened like a heartbeat' has direct reference to Billy's reactions and fears. Here there is an effective telescoping of time – we feel that a long time has passed, but in fact school is still on. Billy jumping up and down is comic-pathetic, his mingling with his group the hope of security. As usual he is on the receiving end from Gryce, though there is further comedy in Gryce losing his balance as he tries to hit him again. Barry Hines conveys exactly the interview situation both outside and inside the medical room, the interaction between boys and their parents. Billy's flirtation with the fire alarm case shows his tendency always to court danger.

The interview is another comic-pathetic sequence, with Billy automatically pigeon-holed as a potential manual worker since he has no idea what he wants to do. Just as education fails, so does job guidance. Billy's determination not to go down the pit registers his independence, his fear of being dragooned, of being shut in instead of experiencing the nature he loves; the question on his hobbies has an ironic force, since training a hawk has no market or job value. When Billy goes to the shed there is the speed of movement again, the physical movement as he searches for Jud and Kes, the mental movement of panic. The lure being wielded alone, without the presence of the bird, is pathetic; Mrs Rose's confirmation of Jud's mood when he knows that the horses he bet on won – and the bet was not placed – a terrible sickening crunch for Billy, who suspects what Jud has done. The re-iterated name of the bird, the call like a scream, shows the torment of the boy – a boy of fifteen, vulnerable, unprotected, alone apart from the bird he loved. So powerful is the description that as Billy nears the woods they seem to become a presence, a face, while the rain is magnified into millions of drops to complement the hopeless sodden mood of the boy. The description of Billy's running search is superb, full of small unobtrusive images which reflect the author's imaginative identification with the boy in his adversity.

Billy's return home and his confrontation with Jud is very poignant. Jud's mental age, his recourse to violence, the inadequacy of Billy's mother, Billy's own need for love and his turning to violence himself in his suffering and frustration, all these are conveyed with immediate and unforgettable visual and physical power. The discovery in the bin is pure pathos; the pride of physical power has been reduced, but Billy's love and tenderness are shown in his smoothing the feathers of the dead Kes into place. The ten quid–bird altercation shows the different standards – money for booze and other birds on the one hand, love and training on the other, with Billy's mother crowning her own apathy and sordid standards with the phrase 'it's only a bird'. Billy's acrobatics get him out of physical trouble, with his swinging the dead hawk as deterrent a grotesque gesture of defiance.

The journey to the deserted cinema is the story of Billy's life. He traverses all his known areas and, in the cinema, the area of the known and loved past before it was shattered by his mother's adultery. His breaking in is a pathetic attempt to recover that past, and the sordid deterioration of the place, with its smells of 'cat piss', is irradiated by the quality of Billy's memory. Note the single-word effects which are cinema credits, and note the return to reality which is ennobled by the simple gesture of burying Kes. The ending is almost unbearable in its poignancy, and there is a deliberate sub–text which implies that such are the frustrations on all levels for a boy like this that he will continue to be a victim, a delinquent, an outsider who never fits and whose potential, shown with the training of Kes, will be forever lost.

109 **driftwood** i.e. driven by water, floating in stream or river.

109 **the pieces of an abandoned game** In view of the cloth, draughts or chess is being suggested.

109 **Toby Jug** These are varied in design, but generally embody an old man wearing a three-cornered hat.

109 **bevelled** Square edges made sloping.

109 **.22 calibre** Internal diameter measurement of a gun.

109 **odds I take it, evens I don't** A reference to Jud's bet of two half-crowns.

109–10 **hairlines . . . dividing the face like a hot-cross bun** A fine image, the contrast between the menace of the gun and the harmlessness of the bun indicating one of the paradoxes of life – one moment security, the next moment, death.

110 **panned** Moved the gun around, brought the sights to bear upon.

110 **shuttering** This conveys the movement and the sound of scratching.

111 **scroamed** Scrambled, climbed awkwardly.

111 **A grey pom-pom with a black bib . . .** There is a vivid and poetic sharpness here which captures the appearance of the bird – the fluffy round ball of the head and the grey front. The following sentences further amplify this.

111 **pinpoint the intersection** i.e. with the sights focused on the sparrow's chest.

111 **kick back** The recoil of the airgun.

112 **on a vertical plane** i.e. upwards.

112 **like a day-tripper paddling at the seaside** Again the rather pathetic holiday image.

113 **throw up ... impetus** Lift herself ... the force of her movement.

113 **like a top matador his cape** An apt comparison with bull-fighting, since the matador appointed to kill the bull has to display exceptional skill comparable to that being shown here.

113 **to pay out** To stretch and lengthen.

113 **shortened her stoop ... to ring up high** The swoop of the hawk ... rising in flight.

114 **ruttling** Rustling, perhaps stroking.

114 **scaled ... spanned** Having scale ... spread.

115 **puffed away like fairy clocks** i.e. like dandelions which have seeded.

115 **quills ... like ash keys** The comparison is with the winged seeds of the ash tree.

115 **snuffled** With a sniffing sound.

115 **a purply-brown pad; the heart, a slippery pebble** Notice the immediate effect of the contrast of textures – they are all the same to the kestrel.

115 **knobbled** i.e. in small knobs.

115 **the tarsi** The shanks of the sparrow's legs.

116 **to feake ... as a strop** To wipe (the beak) after feeding ... as a sharpener.

116 **a little blinder** Exceptional, wonderful.

116 **maggies** Magpies.

116 **T'others weren't in t'same street** The others weren't as good, weren't in the same category.

117 **just like a pair of plus-fours** Mr Farthing thinks in terms of knickerbockers (often worn by golfers), the overhang being produced by increased length.

117 **when it's got it over** When it's superior to.

117 **Scarborough** This is linked to 'when we used to go away', that is, when Billy's Dad took the family on holiday to this Yorkshire resort. This further underlines the pathetic quality of the other seaside references.

118 **pointed two fingers at his temple ...** His way of showing that he was in the wrong, stupid, to make a noise.

118 **carry over** Continue.

119 **she's doin' me a favour just lettin' me stand here** A moving acknowledgement of respect, admiration, awe; the qualities which Kes inspires and which lift her beyond the 'pet' category.

119 **a fender of sand** i.e. in the shape of a guard.

119 **'If men were as much men as lizards are lizards they'd be worth looking at'** Barry Hines shares Lawrence's recognition of the essential independent identity of each animal. The poem referred is to be found in *The Complete Poems of D. H. Lawrence Volume II* p.259 (Heinemann 1957).

120 **a kink** A change, difference.

120 **the final fade** The end.

120 **snuff dry** The comparison is with powdered tobacco, which is sniffed.

121 **like a little standard** i.e. an upright support.

121 **as worn and shiny as a snotty sleeve** The simile implies something unsavoury, dirty, rather like the betting shop itself.

121 **shales** Kinds of clayey stones, easily split.

121 **like skins of moulting animals** The simile suggests a kind of death, the loss of something, and this by association connects with betting – a moral death in itself.

121 **dead dock** Coarse, weedy herb, a remedy for nettle stings.

121 **rose-bay spears** i.e. from the willow-herb.

122 **heads I take it . . .** An echo of his previous indecision with regard to the bet. It is 'heads', but temptation is too great.

122 **a lock-up shop** i.e. shop not used as residence.

123 **wedged like a cartilage** Finely observed comparison, cartilage being elastic tissue gristle in man.

123 **Hey up . . . that's a grand place to be parked** An exclamation at finding Billy directly in his path.

123 **studying form** Considering the past performances of horses running in the race.

124 **S.P.** The starting price, final odds at the start of a race.

124 **top weight** Carrying more weight than the others (in terms of the jockey or additional weights as a handicap).

124 **No form** Has not been successful.

124 **wi' a lad** With an apprentice, trainee, not a top professional jockey.

125 **dollop** A clumsy, shapeless lump.

125 **the big shuttlecock** Cone-shaped bag, the same shape as the shuttlecock used in the game of badminton.

125 his eyes as grateful as the five thousand See Mark 6, 34–44 for the account of the miracle.

126 gobbed them Swallowed them hastily, took them in lumps.

126 cardboard smilers Cut-out heads of girls advertising the permanent waving.

126 Same story, different players Each class doing the same thing – but each room with a different class

127 A voice from the gods From on high, as from the gallery (of a theatre).

127 spangling Glittering, sparkling.

128 A sitting duck along the top of the cupboards Jud's face is seen moving like a target at a shooting range in a fairground.

129 bobbles Blobs, blotches.

129 The teacher closed his novel An example of unobtrusive irony – the teacher has not been teaching but reading for his own pleasure.

130 little-man Crouched down, bowed.

130 Therefore AB . . . five times . . . Like a wall . . . These are stray phrases from the different classrooms which he passes.

131 meshed Having a network of wire.

131 like branches of the beanstalk Jack finds much that is good – the singing harp for instance – at the top of the beanstalk, but the imaginative association set up by this reference is a grim one – we think of Jud as the giant.

132 tigging it Touching it lightly.

132 skiddled Hurriedly fled.

132 as snug as a bug, as warm as toast, as safe as houses The clichés are used ironically here, for the refuge is only a temporary security.

132 a cat-landing i.e. on all fours, the right way up.

132 sneck Latch.

132 like pennies from heaven The title of a very popular song in the late 1930s. They are blessings in that this rain may afford Billy a chance to escape.

132 the grain of the tin Here, apparently, the slope.

133 No birds sang A deliberate echo of Keats's *La Belle Dame sans Merci* 'The sedge is withered from the lake/And no birds sing'. Symbolically, it anticipates the death of the hawk.

134 batted Hit.

134 the invisible man Filmed, and made into a television series, the original may be traced back to H. G. Wells's *The Invisible Man* (1897).

135 **manoeuvred a horseshoe course** i.e. moved in a curve.

135 **on t'bins** On the dustbins, a dustman.

136 **stratum** Layer.

136 **scuffs ... sabres** Rubs ... long curved marks.

137 **tinked it** Simple onomatopoeic effect.

139 **Higher National ... even degrees** i.e. advanced qualifications in practical and academic subjects.

139 **Meccano sets** Miniature parts from which engineering models can be constructed.

140 **like a cat on hot bricks** Restless, nervous.

140 **square glasses ... a flying V bird** The sketch is a comment in itself – it caters for middle-class careers, and the kind of boys who would be chosen for them, and not in any way for 'outsiders' like Billy.

141 **snubbed** Cut off.

141 **like a thrust out tongue** The comparison anticipates the fact that he has been made a fool of.

141 **No birds called ...** A considered pathetic echo of 'No birds sang' on p.133.

142 **welcher** Someone who clears off without paying.

142 **over a tenner to draw** He would have won ten pounds.

143 **as crisp as a kite-tailing** An imaginative association with an innocent pastime, running with a kite and getting it to fly.

143 **fused like a Catherine wheel, and unwound as a rocket** The comparison is with fireworks, but there is no joy, no ecstasy here.

144 **like the top man of a pyramid of tumblers** i.e. acrobats forming up or finishing their act in the shape of a pyramid.

144 **trajectory** Flight.

145 **lattice work against the sky** A pattern, with the light behind.

147 **then back to the comic** An ironic but pathetic confirmation of Jud's mental age.

147 **in this lot** In this downpour.

148 **What's goin' off?** What is happening?

149 **for a price** i.e. the right kind of odds.

149 **broddle** Poke about.

149 **the poker like the Daily Express knight** The red knight, front page, top right-hand corner, has always been there, and is still there in the tabloid version today.

149 **tried to bury his face in her** This underlines Billy's pathetic need of love, care and support – all of which are lacking in Mrs Casper.

150 **as though the wing was a feathered instrument, its note too soft for human hearing** A superb moment of poetry and pathos, the language crystallizing feelings which Billy could not express in this way but giving a sublime quality to his feeling for Kes.

151 **You can get another can't you?** The phrase expresses complete inadequacy and failure to understand.

152 **like a maypole hanger** Originally the pole with its ropes for May Day celebrations, but probably the iron equivalent which is found in many children's playgrounds in parks today.

152 **holding the hawk by the feet ... Its wings opened** A terrible moment, grotesque but moving, for Jud is at least being confronted by the death he caused.

152 **verticals** i.e. the slats of the gate.

155 EVEN FOR THE SALE OF BRISTOL Cigarette advertisement of an unusual kind.

156 THE PALACE Typical name for the kind of cinema that sprang up in the 1920s and 30s; many of them have now been converted to bingo halls or are just derelict.

156 **arabesque** Fanciful, ornate lettering.

156 **façade** The face of the building towards the street.

156 **Graeco-Arabian** i.e. showing Greek-Arab architectural influence.

156 **fluted** Grooved.

157 **stalls** Downstairs seats in the theatre or cinema.

158 **stippled** See note p.19.

158 **cones** Effect of shape against the light.

159 **Big Billy ... Big Kes** The fantasy existence of fame in the cinema world that was once so real to him when he went with his Dad is all that Billy has left now. This is one of the saddest moments in the story. The repetitive 'no contact' indicates that he is losing touch with the rich immediacy of his created 'film' and, of course, with Kes.

160 **Somebody walking over his grave** A spontaneous shiver, here perhaps caused by memory – of his father, whom he loved, and of Kes, whom he loved.

Revision questions on Section 4

1 Write an essay explaining what you find interesting about the conversation between Billy and Mr Farthing.

2 How far do you think that Billy is to blame for what happens to Kes? Give reasons for your answer.

3 Show how Barry Hines creates and sustains an atmosphere of fear in the last section of the novel.

4 Write an account of (a) the interview or (b) Billy's search for Kes.

5 Write an account of the parts played by (a) Jud and (b) Billy's mother in this last section.

Barry Hines's art in *Kes*
The characters

Billy

Billy stood up, a mud pack stuck to each knee. He pulled his shirt sleeve round and started to furrow the mud with his finger nails. 'Look at this lot. I've to keep this shirt on an' all after.' (p.96)

Billy is the centre of all our attention and sympathy in *A Kestrel for a Knave*, his essential spirit a triumph over his under-sized, under-privileged and under-nourished state. Seen at its lowest level, his is the spirit of survival – stealing, trying to keep from being found out, being cheeky, being tired, having no direction in life. At its highest it is revealed as a determination to acquire the kestrel, to train it properly, and to exult in its achievement as well as his own. His home-life – the term itself reads sadly here – is brutalized by Jud and his wayward, uncaring mother; his paper-round ensures that he is too tired to stay awake all day in school and therefore he is constantly in trouble. He is ill-clothed (with no PE or football kit), ill-fed and unloved. He only establishes human contact with one person during the course of the action, and that is his English teacher Mr Farthing, who takes an unexpected interest in the basic training of Kes and comes to see both Billy and the kestrel in action.

Education washes over Billy; the only happiness he has known belongs to the past, the large pleasure of sitting in the pictures with his Dad. This departed, he finds an ecstatic and absorbing interest in the present; this relates entirely to Kes, and Billy's patience and dedication reveal his innate capacity for discipline and experience, a capacity which his teachers have failed to foster, and which Billy himself only learns to articulate in a rush of pride.

It says much for Barry Hines's identification with his character's needs and sufferings that we never for a moment fall out of sympathy with Billy. He steals chocolate, eggs and an orange drink; his newspaper delivery is desultory, to say the least. He fails to place Jud's bet; he tells lies, which stress his defensive attitude towards life. He knows that the small world in which he lives is against him, and his reaction is either to take it on in desperation, or to clown his way through the situations in which he finds himself. There is no more scathing commentary on the vain posturings of Mr Sugden than Billy's self-absorption at the other end of the pitch:

> He hand-over-handed it to the middle and rested, swinging loosely backwards and forwards with his legs together. Then he let go with one hand and started to scratch his arm pits, kicking his legs and imitating chimps sounds (p.97).

Billy is a natural clown and, with his clothes here cut in the Chaplin mould, he resembles that great silent comedian who was so ill-used within his celluloid world. Billy is resilient, but even his capacity to bounce back is undermined by the kind of life he is forced to lead. He is sensitive but, until Mr Farthing encourages him to talk in class, largely inarticulate. His appreciation of nature, unsentimentalized, is moving and real, and it is in nature that he finds a quality of life which is lacking in his own. Thus his 'stealing' of Kes is in itself an act of rebellion and a movement towards love; he is rebelling against the restrictions which tie him to a meaningless, frustrating life at home and in school. His only outlet, as he reveals to Mr Farthing, has been the rearing of other creatures and a delight in their lives before he takes Kes.

Billy is never less than real, but he is also the symbol of the underdog and outsider; he is the 'loner' who acquires for himself what education cannot give him – a pride in achievement, a love of mastery and of giving outside a world which has mastered him and given him but little. Naturally he is badly treated by his fellows, who take his difference, his separateness from the gang as uncomplimentary to their own conditioned delinquency; they bait him mercilessly and, moreover, Billy is very small and can easily be picked on. The result is a catalogue of misery, and from the heart's core of that misery Billy writes 'A Tall Story' (p.73), the anguished expression of what he would like to replace his present reality. The denial of creature comforts has eaten into his small soul; in the story he longs for a large house on the moors, with carpets and central heating, breakfast in bed, the return of his father (just as he remembered him), Jud permanently in the army, the teachers at school all nice to him (Billy); his mother not going to work any more, and fish and chips for tea and supper. Billy's inaccuracies of expression, too, are revealing; he has not been able to absorb the fundamental disciplines of writing, yet his expression, strongly individualized, has an unformed merit that speaks to the reader directly, simply, effectively.

His 'tall story' is one form of escape; another is the *Dandy*, which Billy reads while on his paper-round; another is the vision he has of himself and Kes as stars in the desolate cinema, while the other, linked with this last, is the memory of his Dad. All these serve to underline the contrast with the reality – the poverty, physical, emotional and mental – which is his daily tribulation. Consider Billy's exchanges with Mr Sugden in the changing-room (p.89). The fact that Billy does not wear underwear is of course seen by Sugden as scant excuse for breaking the inviolable rules, and Billy's torture at his hands begins:

He stepped into the shorts and pulled them up to his waist. The legs reached halfway down his shins . . . Boys pointed at them, shouting and laughing into each other's faces . . . (p.89)

Billy is indeed a 'brave little clown'; the Artful Dodger of *Oliver Twist*, sentenced by the magistrate, is not braver. But the above quotation underlines the fact that Billy *has* to play the clown, that it is a pathetic refuge from what amounts to his daily suffering. If we consider the 'joke' level of Desperate Dan, we can see why Billy snatches a few moments with him, for grotesque fooling, an easy laugh. What more can one want from a life that yields so little?

The answer to the question varies from individual to individual; for Jud it is betting and boozing and 'birds', for MacDowall and his gang the loitering that promotes provocation and petty thieving. But Billy has a questing spirit, and translates his wishes into practical action – action, ironically, sparked off by Jud's drunken return on that Saturday when Billy, alone in the house, is absorbed in *A Falconer's Handbook*. Yet Kes is not reduced by captivity; rather she is enhanced. The training and the rewards are shared by boy and bird. Billy is the genuine enthusiast, the amateur who makes himself professional and discovers his own deeper needs in the process. Listen to his voice when he talks of training Kes (p.67).

Billy's humanity, his concern for the hawk, is, like his creator's, never in question. This is all the more remarkable in that there appears to be nothing in his background, save the memory of his Dad, which would give him such a strong moral centre of action. Consider the aftermath of his early-morning exchange with Jud (pp.8–9). The only warm place he finds is in his own heart, and then in the instinctive and trained responses of Kes. I do not intend here to trace Billy's reflexes and the many facets of his character, since this would needlessly extend an outline to a booklength study. Like the author, the reader lives *with* Billy throughout the story; he is our sympathetic pivot, and our emotions turn, so to speak, on his. Overall we are forced to accept the assertion, sometimes overt, sometimes muted, that society and education fail, that what a boy finds within himself is more important than what is thrust upon him. Billy follows his instincts as Kes follows her training, and those instincts reveal a deep-down humanity which the sticks and stones of home and environment have been unable to injure.

Billy is resilient, clowning, persecuted, on the receiving end, scarred physically and morally by what he has to endure; but the capacity to endure, and to find something worthwhile beneath the endurance, is commonly called 'character'. It is not the 'character' of the well-set-up boy in the pamphlet which Billy sees at the interview with the Youth Employment Officer; that kind of character has the conditioning of home and school unquestionably on the right side with the right social milieu and the appetite for conformity which ensures that a person will 'get on'. Billy's character cannot be measured by conventional standards, since he does not conform in dress, speech, habits or educational attainment; his character is derived from his nature. His discovery of Kes is his education, his training of her his integrity, her murder the depths of his disillusion. Use what I have said above as a guide to your own discovery of Billy; you will, if you read closely and imaginatively, find much more than I have said here. You may find yourself moved to anger, frustration, outrage, by Billy's various plights; you may find yourself in part at least understanding why it is that society has no time for the kind of boy that Billy appears to be. You may find yourself appalled by his home circumstances, and because of them have a strong fellow-feeling for him. Do not, in your reading, forget that he is a small boy; old enough to be interviewed for a career (what career?), young enough to need warmth and security, and to give love and security – unsentimentalized, real – to Kes. There are many portraits of children in literature from Oliver

Twist onwards, and children in literature, like children in films or plays, all too frequently suffer from idealization, an excess of goodness (or badness), a lack of reality, a cloying approval. Billy is not such a portrait; Billy is, movingly, painfully, a life.

Jud

He fluffed the bob at the front of his hair and walked out whistling ... 'Hel' me ge' undresh, Billy. Am pish. Am too pish to take my trouser off.' (p.38, p.40)

Jud is Billy's half-brother, and his character need not be dwelt on for long. He is a bully, a gambler, a drunkard, on the make sexually. Billy suffers at his hands physically – Jud has a kind of casual cruelty – for he thumps Billy in the kidneys, baits him and teases him, returns to collect his snap, and then goes off to the pit. He prides himself on his success with 'birds', and makes Saturday night the crown of his week, generally returning home drunk; on these occasions Billy has to cope with him and remove his clothes, and once he punches Jud. This action serves a positive purpose, since Billy flees from imagined retribution and sets off for the farm in the darkness, later secreting the eyas kestrel in his pocket after making a careful selection. Jud has previously thumped Billy for talking overmuch about the kestrels, and thus his return to the bedroom that night, (p.39), inadvertently provides Billy with the greatest pleasure he is ever to know.

   For most of the action of the story we are aware of Jud, but only when Billy returns home at lunchtime and finds the note and the five shillings for the double on CRACKPOT and TELL HIM HE'S DEAD does Jud begin to bulk large again. His presence now stalks Billy's actions in the sense that, knowing Jud, we know only too well what is likely to happen. After a threatening appearance at school Jud, according to his own story, merely intended to let Kes go but, being badly scratched and lacerated by the kestrel, kills her and puts the body in the dustbin. To Jud, the £10 he ought to have won is more important than Billy's hawk. When Billy comes back after his long search for Kes, Jud is reading a comic. What this implies is, of course, a moral and emotional immaturity which makes a necessity of revenge, the destructive urge of the bully who knows that those weaker than himself have no reply.

Mrs Casper

Every time she brushed her palms down the front, her breasts flubbered underneath. (p.37)

Billy's Mum is a positive character only when her own interests are threatened. She calls Billy 'love', but the term is meaningless. When we read Billy's account of his returning home with his Dad from the pictures, it becomes obvious that she was promiscuous and that her husband left her because of this. She is also Jud's mother (though he signs himself J. H. on the 'double' note to Billy) and is a casual, sluttish woman depending on her men and 'going out'. She has little maternal instinct, though she is upset by Jud's killing of Kes. Her way of life is disorganized in the extreme; she is always asking Billy to get things for her (p.19). This is symptomatic of her spur-of-the-moment activity. She says that she'll pay for these at the weekend, but we doubt her word. She threatens Billy, but hasn't the means to enforce a threat (she is not exactly active), and she cannot contain Jud. She is vain, always aware of herself sexually and one gets the impression that she rarely, if ever, cooks. Her clothes are scattered everywhere. Perhaps some small particle of guilt adheres to her, for when she goes out in the evening she will leave Billy some small sum (p.39). But this is the denial of responsibility, the substitute for affection; she has time for nobody but herself. Billy is only too aware of this, and his 'tall story' envisages a changed, always at home, domesticated mother who brings him breakfast in bed. The real mother is inadequate on all counts, unequal to the crisis of emotion that the killing of Kes has aroused. This failure is underlined by an equal failure in emotional comprehension when she says to Billy, 'it's only a bird. You can get another can't you?' (p.151).

Mr Farthing

'Now then, Billy, tell me about this hawk. Where did you get it from?' (p.64)

Of the three schoolmasters who play positive parts in the story, Mr Farthing is the most sympathetic, though Gryce pudding has his moments of understanding behind the abrasive exterior he presents to the world of boys. Mr Farthing encourages Billy, sympathizes with the fact that he has been caned yet again, and coaxes from him the story of the training of Kes. He is a good teacher, his informal attitudes and the relaxed atmosphere in which he operates ensuring a positive response from the boys. He stimulates Anderson's exciting – and funny – narration of the tadpole incident and, with a warm understanding of Billy's isolated position, draws him out and into participation. He has a good sense of humour, but is sensitive enough to contain it and not over-play it – witness his 'tall story' joke about Billy which he doesn't indulge when he sees that Billy is not quite following him. His imagination is flexible enough for him to concoct a tall story himself, and although the subject set as an essay is a little obvious, perhaps we are shown Mr Farthing paying a necessary lip-service to the system – written work which can be given a mark, a record of 'education'. He rescues Billy from MacDowall, and it is here that his wisdom in dealing with the basic situation is shown. He hates bullying and the recurring effect of it, but mock-bullies MacDowall in order to make his point and to try to deter him from bullying in the future.

Mr Farthing's natural affinity with the underdog is deepened when he talks to Billy after this incident, and without offending he questions Billy about his life, about his becoming a 'lone wolf' now that he has the kestrel, about his home, about his job prospects. Later he goes to see Billy training Kes, and responds with that generosity and warmth of feeling which are his most endearing attributes. No schoolmaster-schoolboy convention of distance inhibits his utterance. He further responds to Billy's self-acquired expertise, and in addition his aesthetic appraisal dignifies Kes, marks the permanence of beauty, the delight in the experience and the recognition of its quality (p.118). This is the heightened involvement of the imagination in what is moving and real. Mr Farthing offers Billy a lift back to school in his car; Billy refuses, although the barriers between master and boy have been broken down, and sets off on his fateful journey with Jud's money. So long as schoolmasters like Mr Farthing exist there is hope that his kind of individual commitment will transcend the system, and that it will penetrate to those who need the fundamental humanism of education rather than its academic trappings.

Mr Gryce

'As soon as the hymn is announced you're off revving-up ... It's more like a race track in here than an assembly hall!' (p.46)

Gryce pudding is at first sight caricature, but there is a little more to him than that. He rules by the cane, as he has ruled the fathers of many of the boys before him. Times have changed, however, and Gryce does not fully understand the change, though he is able to estimate its effects. His threats are enough to compel silence; his action at any infringement, decisive. The ritual of hymn-signing is enforced until some kind of tone and volume is achieved. His wit is sarcasm, heavy, unfunny, deliberate. Considering that he is presiding over prayer, he is singularly lacking (outwardly) in Christian charity or humility.

He is an inveterate talker, haranguing the 'smokers' union', Billy and the messenger with his reminiscences and his bewilderment:

'I thought I understood young people, I should be able to with all my experience, yet there's something happening today that's frightening, that makes me feel it's all been a waste of time . . .' (p.55)

And in a sense it has, for experience has not sharpened his discrimination, and Gryce dispenses an even-handed justice that breaks the innocent but hardens the guilty. The messenger is sick after the cane (Billy is later to tell Mr Farthing of the unfairness), but although Gryce wields authority he is aware of failure yet has no means of combating it. He falls back on a common contemporary cliché: 'You're just fodder for the mass media' (p.56), admitting that there is no solution apart from the cane. In effect he is a slave to the system which he is not prepared to set about changing.

Mr Sugden

He was wearing a violet tracksuit. The top was embellished with badges depicting numerous crests and qualifications, and on the breast a white athlete carried the Olympic torch. (pp.86–7)

The above description is sufficiently definitive of Sugden, the outward show and ornamental shell covering a hollow centre. Just as Billy escapes to the fantasy world of the *Dandy*, so Sugden lives in a fantasy world – the image of the great athlete and games player, bending the rules to make the fantasy come true, wearing the colours of famous football teams and identifying himself with famous players in them. The boys play up to this knowing that it is the surest way of getting something of a game themselves. But allied to Sugden's vanity and self-indulgence there is a sadistic streak, and Billy is the natural foil for him. He forces Billy to wear the grotesque shorts, kicks the ball brutally at him after he (Billy) has let in a goal; he shows his cowardice when a dog strays on to the field, and finally forces Billy to have a shower although he hasn't got a towel. Sugden has an audience in his own consciousness, and always plays to it. He may be compared with Jud – intent on having his own way, asserting his will, needing to win (as Jud needs a 'double up') and taking delight in tormenting a small boy. These are all the more degrading in Sugden, since he at least, unlike Jud, has had the advantage of an education. There is something humorous in the delineation of Sugden, but there is also something menacing; the contrast with the boys he teaches is evident, for their standards are straighter, essentially more honest, than his. It is one of the fine ironies of the book that Billy shows more responsibility and dedication to Kes than Sugden does in the carrying out of his duties.

Minor characters

These only take part in sections of the story, and merit only a passing comment here.

MacDowall is a bully cast in the Jud mould (probably frightened of Jud though), given to teasing and innuendo, secretly jealous that Billy's affinity and occupation with Kes have turned him away from the road of a shared delinquency. *Anderson*, who tells the story of the tadpoles, has a surprising fluency when stimulated into talking by Mr Farthing, while of the other boys *Tibbutt* stands out for his propitiation of Mr Sugden, though it is based on his knowledge of the latter's weakness and does not involve him (Tibbutt) in any loss of face. The only other teacher, Mr Crossley, has a caricature name, and his actions show him to be dully sarcastic and a ready subordinate to Mr Gryce. The *farmer* and his *daughter* come alive briefly when Billy makes his early-morning expedition to the farm; initially suspicious of

Billy, the farmer proves himself on closer acquaintance to be gruff but kind-hearted, apparently telling Billy off, but perhaps impressed by his interest. *Mr Porter*, owner of the paper-shop, is a typical sarcastic, complaining man who tries to take his worries out on Billy. These characters are all part of the plot, and they are seen vividly and immediately, however brief their appearance. They give to *A Kestrel for a Knave* the adhesive of consistency.

Themes

A number of themes relevant to our own time, in fact a part of our own time, are given a considered stress. These themes are carefully structured to give a nice balance between the personal – Billy and the kestrel – and the wider implications which deal with education and society. Seen simply at one level, the reader is forced to contrast the expertise which Billy patiently and humanly acquires in his training of Kes, with his lack of achievement in any aspect of formal education, even games, where those who are unacademic frequently compensate by making at least a physical mark. Billy is a thief, a liar, exists in degrading conditions, has no purpose or direction in life and, apparently (see the interview with the youth Employment Officer) no hope for the future. The thematic emphasis falls squarely on the kind of background and foreground which helps to form such a boy and to give him an unremitting pessimism of outlook. The quality of social and moral life on an amorphous estate (here set in the North) is unerringly probed; its children are fed into the large comprehensive school of the area, where the morality chiefly consists of violence, gossip and pettiness. Teachers exact punishments and in many cases enforce a code without understanding, compassion or concern, though here it must be acknowledged that one teacher, Mr Farthing, penetrates the heart of Billy's particular matter, first encouraging him to talk about the kestrel and then going to see the training of it himself. Mr Farthing is vital to the overall conception of the novel, for his following-up of Billy's talk by a visit represents the entrance of humanity and compassion into a boy's world which is largely devoid of both.

A reading of *First Signs* (1972), which describes the return of a graduate to his 'roots', the mining area in the North where he grew up, reflects Barry Hines's uncompromising attitude towards those aspects of contemporary education which are negative because of misplaced emphases:

'Do you know, we're not touching the majority of kids in our schools, we're not getting anywhere near them. All we're concerned with is the academic minority. The rest just trail along in their wake, following diluted academic syllabuses which are completely irrelevant to their lives ... And the potential, Dad, the wasted potential. The talent that just withers through boredom and lack of care.' (p.114)

Billy is untouched, 'wasted potential', his capacity for boredom infinite until he discovers and cherishes Kes. The central theme of the novel is the terrible impersonality which is stamped on modern life, the failure of the system to encourage the development of individuality; in his own self-discovery Billy reaches towards the ecstasy of fulfilment in his dedication and discipline with Kes, but he does it despite the system, which is more concerned with providing betting-shops for its adults than the first-hand experience of nature which Billy finds.

But let there be no misunderstanding of Kes. The kestrel is a predator, the living witness that Tennyson was right when he described nature as being 'red in tooth and claw'. But what Barry Hines is saying is that it is proud, living by its laws and the laws of nature: it is not subject to the meaningless and ephemeral excesses of, for example, drinking, gambling, licentiousness. The kestrel lives by the finer system of discipline, training, control and care; in contrast, the smaller system of education encourages frustration, degradation, apathy. Billy provides meat for Kes, and the hawk devours a sparrow with exact and ruthless efficiency, logical, scientific and clean; the school provides scant meat for Billy, who dozes in lessons, absents himself whenever possible, is a clown at games, and has not been stimulated towards a career. Even that dubious amenity provided in the shadow of the school, the playground, is a battlefield where bullies and victims enact with all the ferocity of children their future roles in life. The only escape is in individual fulfilment of some kind – a hobby, a game, perhaps a caring home if you have one to go to. Just as the hero of *The Gamekeeper* (1975) escapes to his life with nature from the drudgery of the steelworks, so Billy's only refuge from an aggressive and frightening world is his pride in Kes.

The themes of *A Kestrel for a Knave* embrace a contrasting attitude towards life: self-fulfilment and discovery as distinct from self-indulgence; a delight in what there is in nature compared with what man has made; a recognition of the evils inherent in modern urban society, and the failure of the present educational system to provide guidance, enlightenment or even relevance to modern problems of living. So far the content is pessimistic, but it would be unfair to the author to neglect that large area of the novel which is concerned with a fundamental, humanitarian concern seen at its best in the development of Billy. Basically, Billy is unheroic material: his moral flaws are evident. Yet he is the centre of all the action, wrapped in the author's concern for him and his kind. Billy's life is variously divided between home, paper-round, school and Kes, and only the latter affords satisfaction and security. The theme of compassion runs throughout, extending to characters who, at first sight, seem unsympathetic; I say 'unsympathetic' because Mr Sugden, with his small vanity, MacDowall, the bully who cannot take bullying, Billy's Mum, with her clandestine Reg making off from the back of the house, and even Gryce pudding, schoolmaster from the past caught up in the trappings of change with which he cannot deal, all appear selfish or inadequate. But such a reading would fail to understand the author's underlying concern for humanity which is reduced by the modern context of life: their circumstances, their need for 'kicks' – fantasy, sex, betting, aggression, even sadism – all arise from within the urban society which has lost direction, lost the essential spirit of life. Even Jud, with his betting, his birds and his comic, has an image but not an identity; his conditioning has made him cock of the walk and victim at one and the same time.

This moral and social commentary – and I do not mean moral in any limited sense – is reinforced by what is, for this reader at least, a superb identification with nature both in its essential beauty and its essential truth. The nearest analogy one can draw is, I think, with D. H. Lawrence, who saw nature as she is without the considered gloss of too much philosophy; Barry Hines does too and, like Lawrence, he infuses his theme with the direct poetry of appraisal (see the section on *Style*). Thus nature, which lies to hand, is contrasted with all the sordid materials which constitute modern life by implication:

Dew drenched the grass . . . crystal splinters. (pp.24–5)

I do not wish to stress here the symbolic effect of this (again see the section on *Style*) but rather the fact that nature is seen, felt, *real*, and that it is reality to Billy. The poetry and the observation blend; it is a moment of first-hand experience for the reader too, and words like 'communion' and 'affinity' can do but scant justice to its quality. That quality is extensive in its range, not merely limpid, as here. Consider, for example, the description of the hawk and its prey (p.28). Here the poetry is sharpened by the cruelty of fact; hawks kill, for themselves and for their young, and Billy, young, unreared, watches. He is to follow nature, and rear a young hawk with the human love and care which is lacking in his own life. Seen in this way, the novel is a positive affirmation of man's humanity and his ability to survive.

Another aspect of *A Kestrel for a Knave* which merits brief attention here (though again, it is mentioned in the section on *Style*) is the humour which is present throughout. Adversity, however black, often conjures the wit or clowning of resilience, and *A Kestrel for a Knave*, with its inherent sadness, is often lifted by the currents of humour which swirl through it. Sometimes this is verbal, but there is always the humour of situation: the elaborate posing of Mr Sugden as footballer extraordinary, Billy shaking the steps and causing Mr Porter to totter, Billy miming, clowning in goal while the ball is upfield, Billy appearing above the partition wall and getting down on the dry side after the Sugden torture. Sometimes the humour is grotesque – the fight in the coke between Billy and MacDowall, for instance – and sometimes it is imbued with that terrible pathos which catches the reader's breath, as, for example, when the innocent messenger is caned; here, again, it is the grim humour of reality. But it is never far away, and I have called it a theme because it is symptomatic of a resilient and sympathetic attitude towards life and its experiences. It further underlines the humanity of the author.

Structure

The structure of *A Kestrel for a Knave* is technically unusual in one way – there are no formal chapter numbers. The effect conveyed is that of continuing experience, rather like that of a film, and one can see at once that it would naturally lend itself to the visual and verbal experience of the cinema. In fact, one of the major techniques of the film-maker – that of the flashback or retrospect – forms an important structural facet of *A Kestrel for a Knave*. The flashback is nearly always used in fiction to explain, to integrate, the individual psychology of character, and *A Kestrel for a Knave* is no exception to this. The first section of the novel describes a typical morning for Billy (not quite typical, since Jud has taken his bike) – the getting up, the bare larder, the paper-round; the petty thieving, a surreptitious reading of the *Dandy* which he has to deliver, return to the paper-shop, then home and a row with his mother. After she leaves, and before he goes to school, Billy goes to the shed in the garden where Kes is kept, and this leads to the flashback – another morning in the past, when Billy had set out to go nesting with friends. They don't appear, and he goes on his own to a nearby farm, spies out the kestrel's nest, and returns to the library to get a book on hawks. Of course, he is not a member, but he goes to a large bookstore and steals a copy of *A Falconer's Handbook*.

The flashback continues with Billy taking the book home, the mockery of Jud and his mother's lack of interest, and then the return of Jud, blind drunk, that night. Billy punches Jud while the latter is in a stupor, and runs away into the night; he goes to the farm and takes an eyas kestrel. Billy returns to the present, finds himself standing in front of Kes in the shed, and then goes to school.

The structure of the novel now begins to unfold, and this third section, the equivalent of a chapter, concentrates on Billy's life at school. The author gives a satirical account of morning registration, and this is followed by an even more devastating description, near parody, of morning assembly as taken by Gryce pudding. Billy takes the opportunity to move back in time to his initial experiences with Kes; it is hardly a day-dream, more an animated re-creation of early joy. He is brought dramatically back to the present by Mr Gryce, and ends up with the smokers and the guiltless messenger, being caned. This school sequence continues with Mr Farthing's lesson on Fact and Fiction, a sequence which contains Anderson's graphic account of the tadpole experience and Billy's superb and articulate description of the training of Kes. Before the break Billy writes 'A Tall Story' which reveals his deepest wishes ('wers are Jud his goind the army my muther saide'), and in the break he is picked on by MacDowall; there is a fight which is not without its comic elements, and this is broken up by Mr Farthing, who shows Billy a warm welcome sympathy. He even wishes to see something of the training of Kes.

But the respite is short-lived. Billy, who hates games and has never had any games kit, is the natural butt for the dangerously childish and sadistic Mr Sugden. Billy is humiliated by the grotesque size of the kit Sugden forces him to wear, and resorts to clowning, mime and make-believe while the 'game' (Sugden-dominated, a vehicle for his own fantasy) is in progress. Unfortunately, anxious to get back to Kes, Billy makes the mistake of letting in the final goal; Sugden exacts revenge by delaying Billy and forcing him to have a shower. Running clearly through the comedy of this sequence is the unvoiced comment that authority which abuses itself is degrading; Sugden has all the gear but none of the fair play, none of the humanity which the boys show to Billy in his suffering.

Now begins what is in effect the final long chapter of the book, though even this is punctuated with retrospect. Billy shoots a sparrow and feeds it to Kes, watched by an appreciative Mr Farthing, who has given up part of his dinner-hour to keep his word to Billy; man and boy are brought close together by the experience and Billy's capacity to explain it in terms which Mr Farthing can respect and even admire ('she's doin' me a favour just lettin' me stand here'). But after this Billy spends Jud's betting money on fish and chips and beef for Kes, going back to school for the afternoon session and dozing. Through a window he sees Jud, but manages to dodge him by hiding in the boiler-room. Nemesis is delayed while Billy has a belated interview with the Youth Employment Officer, but when he returns home he finds that Kes is gone from the shed. The terrible search is followed by the confrontation with Jud and his mother; he escapes and wanders the estate, going into the old Palace cinema, remembering the time when he had visited it with his father. His pride and his nostalgia conjure a picture on the empty screen of Big Billy, Big Kes, his fantasy striving to shut out the terrible reality – small Billy, no Kes, no Dad, no home, Jud still rampant. He buries Kes and goes to bed.

This is the structure of *A Kestrel for a Knave*, a series of episodes in the life of a small boy which constitute a profoundly moving human experience; it is at once aesthetically satisfying and humanly compelling. We begin as we end, with something like despair; man's pettiness, man's selfishness, can destroy what is noble and real. Yet although we have travelled full circle, the taste of something rare, of something precious to the human spirit, remains with us, and despair dies.

Style

My first reading of *A Kestrel for a Knave* was some years ago. I was impressed then, as I am now, with the uniformity of the writing, a consistency of manner which meant that the whole book rang true, with no false notes, no padding, no distortion of experience. Yet within that uniformity Barry Hines employs a variety of stylistic devices; the regional novel, and the use of dialect, goes back to Emily Brontë and beyond. Some of the 'angry' writers of the late fifties and the early sixties used, with forthrightness and sensitivity, the rich source of dialect in their own localities, and indeed it could be argued that the Beatles gave to the Liverpool idiom and the region a universality of acceptance. *A Kestrel for a Knave* is steeped in a consummate use of dialect both at a common and uncommon level.

First and foremost Billy's speech, and that of Jud, his mother and the estate characters, contains a natural infusion of dialect, the everyday usage of 'tha', 'thi', 'gi'o'er', 'owt' and 'champion'. This gives the novel immediate authenticity, a local habitation and a name which are readily recognizable. The book is true to life, more particularly to the sound of life which is called speech. Billy's responses are conveyed through the range of words open to him, and those words have a psychological accentuation, just as Jud's or MacDowall's do. In addition, Barry Hines uses dialect to describe accurately a character or a character's actions: 'ruttling', 'Gobby' or 'mashed', for example, so that there is a linking strand of unity running through the book; the author is true to his characters in the sense that he is using words that they would themselves appreciate. The schoolmasters, by contrast, speak (regardless of accent) what we should, perhaps, call received standard English. Their education has removed them from the idiosyncratic pronunciations and usages of their youth; it has distanced them from the youth they teach. Mr Farthing bridges the human but not the speech gap and this aspect of style acts as a definition of the generation gap, the divisions which separate man and boy. The ear for speech in *A Kestrel for a Knave* is an ear for class and social difference, but it is true to say that all the dialogue in the novel is straight from life. Consider the following exchange (though it can hardly be called that), for in it Barry Hines explores a commonplace of everyday life, that area of non-communication where two people are talking but neither is listening:

'Tha ought to have seen 'em though Jud.'
'A few pints first.'
'An' tha ought to have seen one of them dive down.'
'Then straight across to t'Lyceum.'
'It dived straight down behind this wall. Whoosh!' (p.37)

The two opposing personalities are captured in these words, their opposed ways of life, their standards, their difference of sensitivity and fibre.

Barry Hines is a masterly creator of atmosphere, whether it is the seamy atmosphere of the Casper home, as in the first few pages of the novel, or an atmosphere that is consonant with mood, as in Billy's journey near the end (p.145).

Billy, always in adversity, is made to suffer what he would call 'purgatory', and this time not at the hands of man – an oblique piece of irony – as he strives to find Kes. Here the atmosphere corresponds to Billy's sensations; but there are other, lyrical, moments of poetry in which the atmosphere is expectant, finely descriptive and evocative at one and the same time:

The sky was still clear . . . texture of the sky. (p.28)

In the above quotation, it will be observed that a cumulative effect is achieved; there is a sense of rising tension. The nature of the technique is immediately felt. Conventional sentence structure is discarded in the example above, while single words encapsulate moments. A fine sense of perspective is maintained, and in this kind of description the humanity of the author and his intimate identification with his subject matter are evident.

After the poetic we might consider the factual. Barry Hines has *the logic of the eye*, that meticulous, realistic sense of detail which further authenticates his writing. Take, for example, the kestrel's eating of the sparrow; it is not for the reader with a weak stomach, since its attention to truth is uncompromising and unsparing: (p.115). This is a sustained focus, a marked and important aspect of the author's style which is, essentially, realistic, though there are other aspects which will be considered below. What is described here is intense, clear, definitive: no words are wasted. But when Billy reads the *Dandy* the experience conveyed is also a real one, though different in texture. The cartoon drawings register, largely uncritically, in the mind of a child; the picture sequence is given without the gloss of comment. A short extract will suffice to show the nature of Barry Hines's method:

He attends the wedding . . . BLACK JAKE. (p.15)

Now here the style, with its italics, capitals and exclamations, *is* the comic, another and rather unusual aspect of realistic writing. Other instances occur, when Gryce takes assembly, for example, or when Crossley is calling the register, and even in the football match officiated (if that is the word) by Sugden. It would be true to say that some of these tip over into the satirical, but the author's ear is so true, his eye for detail so keen, that the blend of the actual underpinned by the humorous is achieved without loss of realism.

Consider Billy's continuation of the Shipping Forecast after the name 'Fisher' has been called out at registration: his explanation, the class's reaction and the ensuing dialogue all have the stamp of immediate conversation. The author's ear is tuned also to cliché – 'Third class riding's better than first class walking anyday' (p.14). The limited swearing and innuendo which is commonplace, schoolmasterly parody and sarcasm (p.53 for example) – all the school and domestic scenes of the novel are informed with auditory as well as visual and psychological reality.

The three areas – home, school and nature, with the estate background filling the gaps between – are seen realistically but always with a running allusive and poetic quality in the appraisal of nature. I have referred earlier in this section to the lyrical moments, and these are further reinforced by the use of imagery throughout the novel. The very facility with which this is used, and the contrasting effects achieved by such usage, constitutes an important part of Barry Hines's manner. There is never monotony of style in *A Kestrel for a Knave*, for the author's imaginative flair is such that the reader is exposed to figurative language drawn from many sources of observation and experience. Take, for example, that page or so (49) where Billy is dreaming, during the morning assembly, of Kes; he has unlocked the shed door, and is back with her. Two images on that page stand out:

'faeces as crozzled and black as the burnt ends of matches' 'like someone up on the top board for the first time .

These comparisons are embedded in some fine factual descriptions, but they give some indication of the range and also the packed nature of Barry Hines's style. The dialect word 'crozzled' heightens the first, domestic usage, while the second – from diving, swimming – gives one the outdoor, physical associations which are again an integral part of his writing. There are times when this novel literally vibrates with the imaginative associations set up by metaphors and similes from domestic life, sport, nature, the seaside, from dancing, from individual actions or reactions. The effect is vivid without being pretentious, as if what is sombre or ecstatic, or in between, is subject to the play of the imagination which gives it significance and perspective. Thus *A Kestrel for a Knave* is a series of experiences, as life is, but the animating spirit which is breathed into those experiences reveals a variety of power, of individual appraisal, which raises the quality of these experiences through the quality of expressive suggestions. The attentive reader will look closely at some of these images – and see what effect each category of image, or each individual one, has on our capacity for appreciation. Many of the effects are pointed out in my accompanying textual notes to this commentary, but I have deliberately omitted some interpretations in order to leave the individual student the stimulus of discovery.

Another facet of the style of *A Kestrel for a Knave* is the author's ability to convey narrative tension; the best example in the novel is Billy's journey in search of Kes. Descriptions of journeys undertaken in stress are part of the fabric of nineteenth-century fiction; we remember Jane fleeing from the still-married Rochester in *Jane Eyre*, Bill Sikes's journey into Hertfordshire and back after the murder of Nancy in *Oliver Twist*, Hetty Sorrel's search for Arthur Donnithorne in *Adam Bede*, and above all, perhaps, the retreat of Tess and Angel Clare to Stonehenge in *Tess of the D'Urbervilles*. Graphic narrative art, dramatic, placing the reader within the experience of character, is present in all these, and it is true to say that Billy's vain hunt for Kes in the agonizing sequence which describes it is of their kind and, indeed, their quality. From pages 142 to 147 the mood felt by the reader is at once taut and tremulous with apprehension and fear. Fifteen times the name 'Kes' is repeated in these pages. Perhaps we should add that the last one of those calls is like a sob. Billy, despite being saturated, is not at the end of his physical resistance, as he is to demonstrate, but he is almost at the end of his emotional tether. Through the style Barry Hines conveys both the physical and emotional movement, with here the short statements at the beginning of these sentences qualified by the physical frustration, drawn out, in the later parts of them (p.146).

This introduction to the style of *A Kestrel for a Knave* embraces some of the main aspects, but the enquiring and thoughtful reader will doubtless find others. There is an easy mastery of dialect and dialogue, the ability to create and sustain atmosphere, the poetry of lyrical wonder and factual clarity; a realism inlaid with satirical or ironic overtones, fine humour in situation, innuendo, repartee, graphic narrative art where style is mood: these are the hallmarks of *A Kestrel for a Knave*. Published in 1968, the book is as readable, exciting and moving as it was then, for its style has an integrity and uniformity which compel our response and, indeed, our identification with its substance and its humanity.

General questions

1 Write an essay on Barry Hines's creation of (a) a happy or (b) a sad atmosphere in *Kes*, quoting from the text in support of your views.

Note-form guidelines for answer

(a) *happy atmosphere* Billy training the hawk in front of Mr Farthing (p.112 onwards in Penguin edition) – the various phases of the lure – the final taking of it – the beauty of the bird – the happiness and pride of Billy in Kes – Mr Farthing's admiration – master and boy in happy interaction – the conversation between them – Kes 'streamlined' – the 'pocket of silence' reference – 'I feel as though she's doing me a favour just lettin' me stand here' – the final quiet sequence in the aftermath of the display. (Make sure that you convey the *delight* of Billy, the fact that Kes is greater to him than any of the other animals he has had, and also the *response* of Mr Farthing, the fact that boy and man are *together* in the shared experience and not apart, as the generations are in school. Here Billy is not outsider or victim, but individual in his own independent right of achievement – and Mr Farthing has the natural generosity of spirit to recognize and encourage this).

(b) *sad atmosphere* use the last section of the novel, and particularly (i) Billy's return home after the unavailing search for Kes – the kitchen – his mother – Jud and the comic – the pathos of Billy unloved – the whirling of the hawk in their faces – the escape, leading to (ii) the whole of the last sequence in the derelict cinema – the thoughts to when it was a cinema visited by Billy and his Dad (use of flashback again) – his return home as child – mother and uncle – Dad leaving with packed suitcase – the Billy/Kes film sequence – Billy emerging from the cinema (sadly, life goes on unchanged apart from the loss of Kes for Billy) – the burial of Kes – last, final, sad (yet sense of reverence for the unique quality of the bird).

2 Write an account, in your own words, of the training of Kes, basing your answer on Billy's talk to the class *and* on his session with the kestrel when Mr Farthing comes to see him.

3 Why do you think Billy is fascinated by Kes and the other animals he has had?

4 What aspects of the novel do you find 'poetic'? Give reasons for your views and quote where appropriate.

5 What qualities in the book make you think that it could be turned into a good film? (Do *not* refer to the film already made of it in your answer).

6 What aspects of Billy's character most impress you? You should refer closely to the book to support your statements.

7 Do you feel that Billy gets what he deserves in the end? Refer closely to the story in your answer.

8 Take any sequence of images used by Barry Hines in *A Kestrel for a Knave* and say how they contribute to your appreciation of the book.

9 Compare and contrast (a) Jud and MacDowall; (b) Mr Farthing and Mr Sugden.

10 Write an account of what seems to you to be the finest episode in the book.

11 Which aspects of *A Kestrel for a Knave* do you find most moving and why?

12 Describe the part played by Billy's mother in the story.

13 What part does *either* fantasy *or* dream *or* other escape activity play in *A Kestrel for a Knave*?

14 Write an essay on Barry Hines's use of dialect in the novel. What does it contribute to your appreciation of the book?

15 How effective is the flashback technique in *A Kestrel for a Knave*?

16 By a careful study of certain sections, say what you think Barry Hines considers to be the important things in education.

17 Write an account – referring particularly to the author's style – of what you consider to be the most exciting episode in the book.

18 What aspects of this novel make you think that it will still be a widely read book in 10 years' time?

19 Write an essay on what you consider are the realistic elements in *A Kestrel for a Knave*.

20 Write on any aspect of the book not covered by the above questions.

Pan study aids Titles published in the Brodie's Notes series

W. H. Auden Selected Poetry

Jane Austen Emma Mansfield Park Northanger Abbey Persuasion
Pride and Prejudice

Anthologies of Poetry Ten Twentieth Century Poets The Poet's Tale
The Metaphysical Poets

Samuel Beckett Waiting for Godot

Arnold Bennett The Old Wives' Tale

William Blake Songs of Innocence and Experience

Robert Bolt A Man for All Seasons

Harold Brighouse Hobson's Choice

Charlotte Brontë Jane Eyre

Emily Brontë Wuthering Heights

Robert Browning Selected Poetry

John Bunyan The Pilgrim's Progress

Geoffrey Chaucer (parallel texts editions) The Franklin's Tale
The Knight's Tale The Miller's Tale The Nun's Priest's Tale
The Pardoner's Tale Prologue to the Canterbury Tales
The Wife of Bath's Tale

Richard Church Over the Bridge

John Clare Selected Poetry and Prose

Samuel Taylor Coleridge Selected Poetry and Prose

Wilkie Collins The Woman in White

William Congreve The Way of the World

Joseph Conrad The Nigger of the Narcissus & Youth
The Secret Agent

Charles Dickens Bleak House David Copperfield Dombey and Son
Great Expectations Hard Times Little Dorrit Oliver Twist
Our Mutual Friend A Tale of Two Cities

Gerald Durrell My Family and Other Animals

George Eliot Middlemarch The Mill on the Floss Silas Marner

T. S. Eliot Murder in the Cathedral Selected Poems

J. G. Farrell The Siege of Krishnapur

Henry Fielding Joseph Andrews

F. Scott Fitzgerald The Great Gatsby

E. M. Forster Howards End A Passage to India
Where Angels Fear to Tread

William Golding Lord of the Flies The Spire

Oliver Goldsmith Two Plays of Goldsmith: She Stoops to Conquer;
The Good Natured Man

Graham Greene Brighton Rock The Power and the Glory
The Quiet American The Human Factor

Thom Gunn and Ted Hughes Selected Poems

Thomas Hardy Chosen Poems of Thomas Hardy
Far from the Madding Crowd Jude the Obscure
The Mayor of Casterbridge Return of the Native
Tess of the d'Urbervilles The Trumpet-Major

L. P. Hartley The Go-Between The Shrimp and the Anemone

Joseph Heller Catch-22

Ernest Hemingway For Whom the Bell Tolls
The Old Man and the Sea

Barry Hines A Kestrel for a Knave

Gerard Manley Hopkins Poetry and Prose of Gerard Manley Hopkins

Aldous Huxley Brave New World

Henry James Washington Square

Ben Jonson The Alchemist Volpone

James Joyce A Portrait of the Artist as a Young Man Dubliners

John Keats Selected Poems and Letters of John Keats

Ken Kesey One Flew over the Cuckoo's Nest

Rudyard Kipling Kim

D. H. Lawrence The Rainbow Selected Tales Sons and Lovers

Harper Lee To Kill a Mockingbird

Laurie Lee As I Walked out One Midsummer Morning
Cider with Rosie

Thomas Mann Death in Venice & Tonio Kröger

Christopher Marlowe Doctor Faustus Edward the Second

W. Somerset Maugham Of Human Bondage

Gavin Maxwell Ring of Bright Water

Thomas Middleton The Changeling

Arthur Miller The Crucible Death of a Salesman

John Milton A Choice of Milton's Verse Comus and Samson
Agonistes Paradise Lost I, II

Sean O'Casey Juno and the Paycock
The Shadow of a Gunman and the Plough and the Stars

George Orwell Animal Farm 1984

John Osborne Luther

Alexander Pope Selected Poetry

J. B. Priestley An Inspector Calls

Siegfried Sassoon Memoirs of a Fox-Hunting Man

Peter Shaffer The Royal Hunt of the Sun

William Shakespeare Antony and Cleopatra As You Like It
Coriolanus Hamlet Henry IV (Part I) Henry IV (Part II) Henry V
Julius Caesar King Lear Love's Labour's Lost Macbeth Measure for
Measure The Merchant of Venice A Midsummer Night's Dream
Much Ado about Nothing Othello Richard II Richard III Romeo and
Juliet The Sonnets The Taming of the Shrew The Tempest Twelfth
Night The Winter's Tale

G. B. Shaw Androcles and the Lion Arms and the Man
Caesar and Cleopatra The Doctor's Dilemma Pygmalion Saint Joan

Richard Sheridan Plays of Sheridan: The Rivals; The Critic;
The School for Scandal

John Steinbeck The Grapes of Wrath Of Mice and Men & The Pearl

Tom Stoppard Rosencrantz and Guildenstern are Dead

J. M. Synge The Playboy of the Western World

Jonathan Swift Gulliver's Travels

Alfred Tennyson Selected Poetry

William Thackeray Vanity Fair

Flora Thompson Lark Rise to Candleford

Dylan Thomas Under Milk Wood

Anthony Trollope Barchester Towers

Mark Twain Huckleberry Finn

Keith Waterhouse Billy Liar

Evelyn Waugh Decline and Fall Scoop

H. G. Wells The History of Mr Polly The War of the Worlds

John Webster The Duchess of Malfi The White Devil

Oscar Wilde The Importance of Being Earnest

Virginia Woolf To the Lighthouse

William Wordsworth The Prelude (Books 1, 2)

William Wycherley The Country Wife

John Wyndham The Chrysalids

W. B. Yeats Selected Poetry

Pan study aids

Published jointly by Heinemann Educational Books and Pan Books

Pan Study Aids is a major new series developed to help school and college students prepare for examinations. All the authors are experienced teachers/examiners at O level, School Certificate and equivalent examinations and authors of textbooks used in schools and colleges worldwide

Each volume in the series:
- explains its subject and covers clearly and concisely and with excellent illustrations the essential points of the syllabus, drawing attention to common areas of difficulty and to areas which carry most marks in the exam

- gives guidance on how to plan revision, and prepare for the exam, outlining what examiners are looking for

- provides practice by including typical exam questions and exercises

Titles available: Physics, Chemistry, Maths, Human Biology, English Language, Geography 1 & 2, Economics, Commerce, Accounts and Book-keeping, British Government and Politics, History 1 & 2, Effective Study Skills, French, German, Spanish, Sociology

Pan Study Aids Check Tests

Books of multiple-choice questions designed specifically to help students revise and prepare for O level and similar exams. Use the magic marker to check your answer – at the end of each question write your answer in one box, then rub over the check box and the correct answer will be revealed.

Each book sets questions of exactly the same format and style as those of the examining boards. These provide a comprehensive revision course, check your knowledge and revision progress, and give essential practice in the completion of multiple-choice questions.

Edward Wakeling
Check Test Maths
By the head of maths/computer studies at Stopsley High School in Luton and examiner for maths for the East Anglia CSE Board.

Colin Clegg
Check Test Biology
The author is lecturer in biology at Bournemouth and Poole College of Further Education and author of *Advanced Biology* in the Pan Study Aids series.

John Clarke
Check Test Chemistry
By the head of science at Alleyn's School in London, also a reviser for JMB O and A level chemistry and author of *Teach Yourself Chemistry*.

J. J. Wellington
Check Test Physics
The author is lecturer in education (physics and computer studies) at the division of education of Sheffield University, formerly head of physics at Daneford Comprehensive School, Bethnal Green, London.

Use the magic marker to check your answers!

Pan Literature Guides

Marguerite Alexander
An Introduction to Shakespeare and his Contemporaries
From the mid-sixteenth century to the closing of the theatres in 1642,
English drama proved the finest flowering of the English renaissance.
Marguerite Alexander's *Literature Guide* examines the themes and
development of Elizabethan and Jacobean drama, going on to explore
the social conditions and literary and folk traditions that combined to
produce the period's unique poetry and drama.

John Cargill Thompson
An Introduction to British Drama 1660–1900
John Cargill Thompson's Literature Guide pinpoints fifty major
landmarks of dramatic writing from the reopening of the theatres
under the Stuart kings, the Restoration plays, through the sophisticated
entertainments of Goldsmith and Sheridan, to the stages of Victorian
England where Wilde and Pinero saw the curtain fall on the last act of
the nineteenth century.

Benedict Nightingale
An Introduction to Fifty Modern British Plays
The last eighty years have seen a constant flow of fine theatre across the
English-speaking stage – from the Edwardian finale of Shaw and
Maugham, through the *entr'acte* of Coward and Priestley, to the new
vision of the 1950s and the radical creativity of the last decade. Benedict
Nightingale takes fifty important and influential plays, examining each
in the context of the wider output of the playwright, and providing a
lively and comprehensive survey of the drama of our times.